State Level Public Enterprises
Past & Present

State Level Public Enterprises

Past & Present

Prof. R.K. Mishra
Ch. Lakshmi Kumari

ANMOL PUBLICATIONS PVT. LTD.
NEW DELHI - 110 002 (INDIA)

ANMOL PUBLICATIONS PVT. LTD.
H.O.: 4374/4B, Ansari Road, Darya Ganj,
New Delhi-110 002 (India)
Ph.: 23278000, 23261597
B.O.: No. 1015, Ist Main Road, BSK IIIrd Stage
IIIrd Phase, IIIrd Block,
Bangalore - 560 085 (India)
Visit us at: www.anmolpublications.com

State Level Public Enterprises: Past & Present

First Published, 2006
ISBN 81-261-2945-X

PRINTED IN INDIA

Printed at Mehra Offset Press, Delhi.

Contents

Preface

This book on the State Level Public Enterprises in India: Past and Present describes the functioning of these enterprises in the various states in the country, their problems and scope for improvement in their working. The book discerns the state specific features of the SLPEs, outlines the issues of convergence related to their performance and points to the reasons responsible for divergence in their employee productivity, modes of privatisation and financing. The book reveals two specific patterns relating to the functioning of these enterprises: one led by the State of West Bengal and the other led by the State of Andhra Pradesh.

The book contains a rich mine of data which provides an edge to the authors in analyzing the performance of the SLPEs. The book incorporates suggestions which could help the various states in improving the performance of these enterprises.

The authors look forward to receive comments and suggestions on the various aspects of the study.

Prof. R.K. Mishra

Ch. Lakshmi Kumari

1

Privatisation of State Level Public Enterprises: A Macro Analysis

*Prof. R.K. Mishra**

Introduction

The State Level Public Enterprises (SLPEs) are an important component of the public enterprise system in India. According to the report submitted by the Study Group on Reforms on State Public Sector Undertakings set up by the Planning Commission (2002), 747 SLPEs had the total investment of Rs. 1,97,105 crore as on March 31, 1999. The investment in theses enterprises as per the Institute of Public Enterprise (IPE) database increased to Rs. 3,06,493 crore in 2002-03. The contribution of the SLPEs to the GDP is about 5 per cent as compared to 10 per cent by the Central Public Enterprises (CPEs). The role of SLPEs can be assessed from the total turnover as a percentage of the Gross State Domestic Product. There was no consistent pattern among states and this percentage generally varied from 1 to 17 per cent of the Gross State Domestic Product, with most states falling in the range of 6 to 15 per cent. Although SLPEs constitute 90 per cent of the total investment of the CPEs, they are more than four times the number of the CPEs. The average investment in an SLPE is 20 per cent of a CPE.

* Dean & Director (I/c), Institute of Public Enterprise, O.U. Campus, Hyderabad-500 007.

However, the SLPEs in terms of the resource use and control depict a different picture as compared to their counterparts in the central sector in that they directly impact the functioning of the state economies and have a greater exposure to the state political systems. The SLPEs are characterized by weak middle management systems as they do not have on their rolls the requisite number of professionally qualified mangers. The top management in these enterprises comprise mostly an IAS CEO and nominees of the state governments drawn from civil services, defeated politicians and political party in power. The financial performance of the SLPEs bears the brunt of these shortcomings. Between the 1991-92 and 2002-03, the SLPEs continued to incur net losses and showed the chronic tendency of accumulating losses. The macro analysis provides in the beginning an overview of the SLPEs in India in terms of various financial parameters followed by the general scenario in regard to their privatisation. The differentiating features of privatisation of the SLPEs vis-à-vis the CPEs have been outlined to bring out the challenges that the various state governments have to meet in reconsidering the retention of their portfolios of the SLPEs. The summing up provides the conclusions to formulate an appropriate policy in this regard.

Origin

The SLPEs have come of age. From a mere 23 in the First Plan period their number increased to 754 as on March 31, 1987. The investment in these enterprises was Rs. 30 crores at the end of the First Plan Period. It shot up to Rs. 13,000 crores as on March 31,1987. Inclusive of the state electricity boards and the road transport corporations, the investment in these enterprises stood at Rs. 46,000 crore and their number ascended to 845. It is interesting to note that the number of the CPEs was 226 and the investment therein stood at Rs. 61,603 crores as on March 31, 1987. Thus, the SLPEs are almost four times the number of the CPEs. They are almost three-fourths in terms of the size of the investment in the CPEs. However, the SLPEs considerably differ from the CPEs in terms of the diversity of operations, origins and objectives. The SLPEs are engaged in a variety of activities ranging from industrial development and financial promotion, trading and marketing, contract and construction services, consumer goods and production of engineering goods to development of backward regions and weaker sections of society, and development and promotion of specific sectors of industry viz., agro-industries, minerals and metals, the small industry and tourism.

The SLPEs owe their rise in numbers to historical factors rather than ideological considerations. Some SLPEs were established by the then princely states and inherited by the new state governments formed after independence. In designing new developmental efforts consideration was given to the fact that there was no local entrepreneurship for taking up large projects. The state governments, therefore, undertook public investments to promote such companies. Many of them started with a view to utilise the locally available raw materials like lime stone for cement or silica for glass works, clay for ceramics, bamboo for paper, etc. Some units were started with a view to meet the local demands for specific goods. In some cases, the state governments were pushed into public investment by the policies adopted by the central government in those days of giving preferential licenses to public sector units. The central government also initiated action in forming joint ventures with the state governments for promotional purposes such as the fisheries development corporations, state finance corporations and state agro-industries corporations. Furthermore, the welfare corporations were started with the explicit objective of helping a particular segment of society which could not have obtained help under the normal market conditions. Many activities which could have done departmentally by the state governments were organised as public enterprises with a view to mobilise investible funds from the national and international financial agencies. An analysis shows that barring a few considered as an instrument of the socio-economic policy of the state governments in a more direct form than the CPEs.

The public policy on approach to economic development differs from state to state. The SLPEs of varied kinds may have to be set up to prop up the rate of economic development in the case of a newly formed state but where the states have involved themselves for quite sometime directly in the productive activities, there is a need to have a fresh thinking on what should and what should not be retained as a part of the SLPEs portfolio. Viewed from the product portfolio of these enterprise, there can not be a strong defence built up in favour of retaining the manufacturing of soaps, detergents, scooters, textiles, cement and light industrial items. The paper and mining industries get qualified by this norm for retention in the SLPEs portfolio. We may go a step further and even suggest the need for turning over the high-tech SLPEs to the private sector as by that time sufficient private incentive should be able to forge ahead to take over such activities from the public sector. The acceptance of this suggestion may free funds to the tune of about 3000 crores from the SLPEs and reduction of losses to be born by the state governments of Rs. 100 crores per annum.

Typology

Table 1 presents the sectoral distribution of the various SLPEs. The various categories in which the SLPEs have been divided include Manufacturing, Financial, and Promotional, Trade and Service, Utility and Welfare sectors. The manufacturing enterprises are followed respectively by promotional, utility, welfare, financial and trading and services enterprises. The manufacturing enterprises dominated the scenario because the various state governments emulated the central government in giving a fillip to industrialization. The trading and services enterprises received an encouragement to provide export thrust and create a suitable infrastructure of services at the state level. The promotional enterprises were set up to orient social activities with an economic tinge at the state level. The welfare enterprises were a new breed of the SLPEs set up to provide economic support to the backward classes of society, comprising scheduled castes, scheduled tribes, minorities, women and handicapped. The table indicates Andhra Pradesh, Assam, Gujarat, Karnataka, Kerala, Maharashtra, Tamil Nadu, Uttar Pradesh and West Bengal showed a preference for manufacturing, promotional and financial enterprises Maharashtra, Kerala and Uttar Pradesh setup a large number of welfare enterprises. The preference for economic and social infrastructure might have been responsible for the respective choice. Andhra Pradesh, Delhi, Karnataka, Orissa, Tamil Nadu and West Bengal has a major share in the utility sector enterprises. The utility enterprises comprised the state road transport corporations and the unbundled power sector enterprises.

Chart 1: All India: SLPEs Categorywise

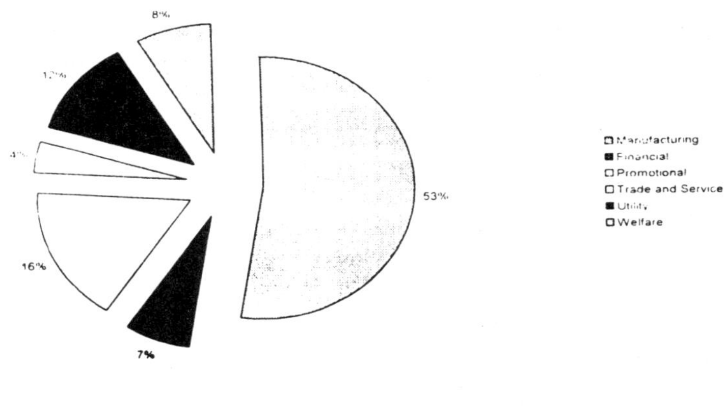

Trading and Service State Level Public Enterprises (TSLPEs)

These Enterprises include marketing, trading and service SLPEs. The state marketing corporations, state export corporations, and state civil supplies and essential commodities supply corporations fall under the mould of this category. Their main objectives vary from marketing of goods produced by small producers undertaking production of perishable and durable consumable items, strengthening economic base of producers by providing financial assistance, modernising their production organisation and marketing of their products to achieve economy in execution of construction works. There were 121 such enterprises with a capital investment of Rs. 1588 crores as on March 31, 1987. Their capital investment doubled over the period 1981-82 to 1986-87. In terms of numerical strength *Kerala*, Bihar and *Karnataka* have these enterprises in two digit numbers. In terms of investment in three digit numbers, Punjab was followed by Haryana, *Bihar*, Karnataka, Uttar Pradesh and Kerala. Against 10 per cent of PBIT on the capital invested the rate of return was hovering around 8.32 per cent in 1986-87 and it was low as 1.61 per cent in 1983-84 to these states. In fact Bihar, Maharashtra and Tamil Nadu earned the distinction of earning a negative rate of return although during the period 1981-82 to 1986-87 in this category of enterprises. These Enterprises had a very low turnover to capital employed ratio. The approach followed in this regard related more to selling than marketing. Most of these enterprises suffered from the glaring incidents of bad cash management. The lingering and increasing overdues and the low inventory turnover ratio coupled with low working capital turnover support this connection. The accumulated losses in these enterprises had eaten away a good chunk of the paid up capital. The handlooms and handicrafts units in the TSLPEs had very low physical achievements, especially in the area of modernisation of looms. They did not export the targeted amount of cotton fabrics although they had a very high export potential. The construction enterprises as a constituent of the TSPLEs were relegated to the status of mere intermediaries as most of these enterprises worked behind the schedules with respect various contracts. The civil supplies and essential supplies corporations were characterised by laxity in procurement and distribution and incurred an extra expenditure on wasteful items leading to losses. In fact, there have been cases when these enterprises embarked upon the schemes without working out their economics and without having any expertise in the connected area. The off-season procurement were made and the style pursued in obtaining the supplies did not reflect commercial poderence on their part. However, it may be admitted here that these corporations are fulfilling a major social objective of mitigating foodgrains shortages in the areas faced with scarcity and providing price-support to agriculturists. It may be difficult to withdraw from this area at this stage. Nevertheless, it will be worthwhile to suggest that these enterprises can hive-off the non-foodgrains procurement activity such as the maintenance of large fleet of trucks, etc. The state warehousing corporations also need to rethink about the relevance of their activities in the present context. It is worth noting that large storage capacities are being developed in the private sector.

A peep into the performance of these corporations raises the question as to whether the various activities pursued by them qualify any more for the retention in the portfolio of the TSLPEs. Coming to the construction corporations it can be pointed out that the time and cost overruns disqualify their continuation furthermore as state corporations. To add, there is sufficient private expertise and initiative available on this front which can easily substitute for the public economic initiative. The construction activity, as a specialised task, requires a large number of proficient technical people and their management which can better be left to the private sector.

Though it is advisable to operate the handlooms and handicrafts corporations in the state sector, the export of their products and internal marketing can better be left to the private sector in view of the quick decisional requirements as the basic characteristic of such an activity. The state trading organisations have lost the gloss during the last decade. They have failed to overcome the market failures in order to help the small producers or consumers and are characterized by high rent extractions due to the monopoly in their trading and wind falls of market fluctuation. Most of the state trading organisations have very little freedom in following market trends and taking up entrepreneurial decisions to promote trade either within the country or outside. Their contribution in the total foreign trade is very insignificant. They are not in a position to checkmate the strategies of their counterparts in the private sector. What to talk of developing countrywide outlets, they have failed to manage even their existing small networks. This analysis brings out very clearly that the TSLPEs will have to reorient their working to match the challenges posed by the dynamic market conditions and their counterparts in the private sector. This will impinge on such enterprises to develop suitable systems and procedures, on the one hand, and discontinue the superfluous activities, on the other.

Financial State Level Public Enterprises (FSLPEs)

These enterprises include in their ambit the state financial corporations, state industrial development corporations, state investment enterprises, state leasing companies, chit funds and banks and institutions for financing the panchayat raj bodies. They are involved in accelerating the rate of industrialisation in the state, removing regional imbalances and promoting growth of tiny, medium and small industries. There were 54 such enterprises with a capital investment of Rs. 5055 crores as on March 31, 1987. Maharashtra had a maximum investment of Rs 831 crores in these enterprises followed by Rs. 616 crores in Uttar Pradesh Rs. 480 crores in Tamil Nadu and Rs. 454 crores in Gujarat and Rs. 437 crores in Andhra Pradesh, one third of the units promoted by these corporations have fallen sick. The disbursements are about 50 per cent of the sanctions in these enterprises. In the case of many such corporations developed regions have received more assistance than the backward regions. They are working mostly as extended arm of the Industrial Development Bank of India engaged in refinancing. Against 9 per cent of the PBIT on capital invested in the years between 1981-82 and 1986-87, their earnings could not exceed 3.29 per cent in any year of the study. Though these enterprises will have to play a great role in the development process, they will have to introduce fundamental changes in their orientation and working. For instance, they will have to formulate speedy disbursement policies to enable them to be eligible for receiving refinance from the Industrial Development Bank of India on their own without approaching the state governments time and again for the renewed equity support. They will have to innovate new schemes keeping in view their clientele. Similarly, considerable effort will have to be made to step up the recovery of overdues. Instead of expanding their work force and depending on their own personnel they will do well to obtain non-essential services from external agencies.

Promotional State Level Public Enterprises (PSLPEs)

The PSLPEs include the forest development corporations, small scale industrial development corporation, tourism development corporations and fisheries development corporations. These enterprises are charged with the responsibility of undertaking the activities assigned to them on promotional basis with both non-commercial and commercial objectives. The small scale industrial development corporations initiated in the 1960s to help the small scale industrialists in terms of supply of raw materials, financial inputs and marketing assistance. These enterprises also take up the manufacture of certain products incidental to their main activities. The forest development enterprises were started in the middle of the 1970s. They have been set up to promote social forestry, conserve and commercially exploit forest produce, develop forest wealth and protect the interests of tribal population living in the forest. The tourism development enterprises also sprung up in the 1970s. Almost all the states in the country have tourism development corporations now. These are engaged in promoting tourism in their respective states by helping private entrepreneurs and taking up many schemes on their own. The fisheries development corporations were set up in the 1960s to help the fishermen engaged in selling fish and allied produce. These enterprises have taken up the manufacture of boats, etc. for the fishermen. In a nutshell, the PSLPEs primarily undertake the non-commercial functions and in the pursuit to do so they have taken up commercial activities to fulfill the role assigned to them. The major objectives of these enterprises include the promotion of economic activities assigned to them through encouraging the private entrepreneurs by direct involvement acting as nodal agencies in their area of operations charged with the responsibility of preparing and implementing the plans for the development of respective activities assigned to them, and continuing to function on a self-sustained basis. As on March 31, 1987 there were 248 promotional enterprises with a capital investment of Rs. 1960 crores. To achieve the ends of public policy, Uttar Pradesh set up 21 such enterprises followed by 20 in West Bengal, 19 each in Karnataka and Kerala, 17 each in Andhra Pradesh and Tamil Nadu and 16 each in Gujarat and Bihar. Andhra Pradesh had a maximum investment of Rs. 263 crores in these enterprises in 1986-87 followed by Rs. 220 crores in Bihar. Rs. 188 crores in Maharashtra and Rs. 157 crores in Orissa. The financial performance of these enterprises was not very promising. The PBIT on capital invested fluctuated between 0.31 per cent in 1981-82 and 1.43 per cent in 1986-87 against the 8 per cent norm for such enterprises. The PSLPEs in Bihar, Manipur, Punjab and Meghalaya had a minus PBIT during the period 1981-82 to 1986-87. These enterprises were involved both in promotional and commercial activities. They did not organise their commercial activities efficiently. However, they will have to play a significant promotional role in the years to come as the development of small industry will continue to be a major plank of the industrial strategy in this country. The forest development corporations in view of the environmental changes and protection of interest of tribal population living in the forest will have a great role to perform in the future. Similarly, the promotion of tourism will be an important economic activity in the state sector in the years to come. The PSLPEs, such as the fisheries development corporations, have a great role and relevance not only in today's socio-economic order. As these enterprises have fallen short of expectations in respect of their non-commercial functions it will be proper on their part to confine their activities to promotional aspects. For instance, there does not seem to be much of the rationale in setting up furniture unit by a small scale industrial development corporation. Similarly, it is worthwhile to ask as to why a fisheries development corporation should set up a boat building plant. Building on the argument further, it will be worthwhile to see as to why the state tourism development corporation should go on building hotel, increasing their fleet of buses and piling up huge assets. These enterprises will do well to exploit the benefits of the networking existing in their own fields of operations.

Welfare State Level Public Enterprises (WSLPEs)

These enterprises are late entrants on the SLPEs scene. Some of these enterprises were set up for the first time during the middle of 1970s by a couple of state governments. However, by the middle of 1980s most of the states of the Indian Union had established these enterprises. The term WSLPEs is omnibus in its nature and difficult to define. In its wider sense, it includes all such enterprises that are engaged in the welfare of the masses of country in general. In the restricted sense of the term it includes only those enterprises which are involved in the upliftment of the scheduled castes and scheduled tribes only. However, for the purpose of this paper the WSLPEs may be said to include the scheduled caste development enterprises, scheduled tribe development enterprises, minority development enterprises backward class development enterprises and area development enterprises. These enterprises have not been set up under a specific form of organisation. A survey of the practices prevailing in different states shows that these enterprises have been established either as the government companies, or cooperative societies or statutory corporations. From a mere 11 in 1975-76 the number of the WSLPEs shot up to 82 in 1986-87. Of the 82 WSLPEs 50 are functioning in 13 states as scheduled caste, scheduled tribe, women development and minorities enterprises. The rest of the 32 WSLPEs are scattered over 8 states as area development enterprises and have been incorporated in the form of government companies. There is no uniformity in the distribution of these enterprises across the states. Uttar Pradesh had a maximum of 16 WSLPEs followed by 12 in Maharashtra, 11 in Madhya Pradesh and 10 in Kerala. The WSLPEs were conspicuous by their absence in Goa, Jammu and Kashmir, Himachal Pradesh, West Bengal, Meghalaya and Orissa. The broad objectives of these enterprises relate to helping the weaker sections of the society to enable them to cross poverty line though a gradual and sustained effort, transforming the economic structure of the weaker sections through the entrepreneurial mode, working for the social upliftment of down trodden strata of the society through working for their educational upsurge, and mobilising the institutional credit for the socio-economic upliftment of the weaker sections of the society. The WSLPEs has an investment of Rs. 471 crores in 1986-87. Uttar Pradesh, Andhra Pradesh, Gujarat and Maharashtra had a lion's share in the investment for these enterprises. These enterprises have been although in the red for all the states taken together during the period 1981-82 to 1986-87. Against the norm of 5 per cent PBIT on capital invested, only Andhra Pradesh, Gujarat, Kerala and Maharashtra could keep head above the water. These corporations were set up to take over the departmental activities of the state governments with the view that their conversion into corporate enterprises would help in providing such activities the commercial orientation. But the performance of these enterprises has betrayed the hopes. The overheads in these corporations were exorbitantly high. Many schemes did not register much progress. The disbursement per beneficiary/scheme was very low. The margin money advanced was not distributed fully. In a give year the recovery of principle and interest had been very low. Further, they were characterised by organisation structures inconsistent with their objectives. Most of these enterprises suffered from the short tenure of managing directors. In that case of the Andhra Pradesh Scheduled caste Cooperative finance corporation in 1988-89 six Managing Directors were replaced within an averaged tenure of about two months. Most of the General Managers and Middle level Managers were deputationists from Government departments with very little corporate understanding. The schemes introduced in a particular year were discontinued very soon. A question may be raised as to why these corporations cannot remove the overlap in their functions and provide better services at reduced costs by curbing down overheads through restructuring. It is worth examining here as to why these corporations should not be reconverted back into government departments in order to bring down the overheads and ensure coordination. Since development of weaker section of society will continue to remain an important concern in years to come, these corporation are expected to play a great role in case they are not reconverted into government departments. The WSLPEs can grow by leaps and bounds and can acquire in that process the requisite commercial tinge if they mobilize considerable finances from the financial institutions.

Financial Performance and Fiscal Impact: Total Investment

The total investment comprises of sum total of the investments in the form of equity and debt capital by State Government and others which includes the Central Government, holding company and financial institutions. Table 2 shows the total investment in the SLPEs. The total investment in these enterprises for all the states taken together increased from RS. 77,729 crore in 1991 to Rs. 306493 crore in 2002-03. The lion's share of about 85 per cent total investment belonged to utility enterprises. The major portion of total investment was shared by Andhra Pradesh, Delhi, Gujarat, Karnataka, Maharashtra, Punjab, Rajasthan, Tamil Nadu, Uttar Pradesh and West Bengal. The Compound Average Growth Rate (CAGR) of total investment for the period 1990-91 to 2002-03 was 12.5 per cent. The investment grew at a slower pace during the period 1990-91 to 1996-97. The growth much faster during the 1997-98 to 2002-03. In 1997-98, the rate of growth of investment was high as it was the closing year of the Eight Plan. In 1998-99, the rate of growth in investment maintained a high tempo as it was the opening year of the Ninth Plan.

Chart 2: All States: Total Investment

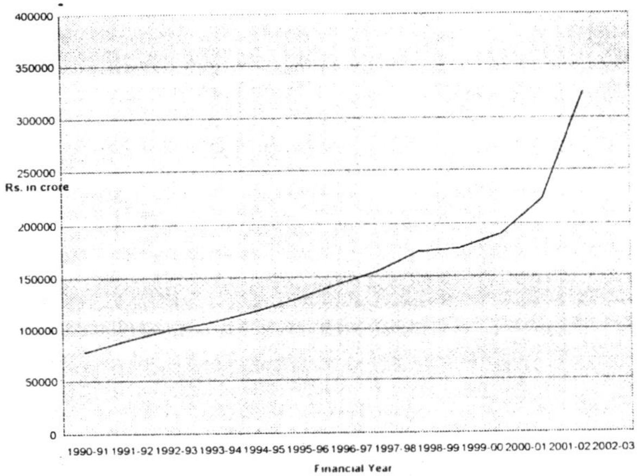

Capital Employed

The capital employed comprises of the sum total of the investment in the next fixed block and working capital. The net fixed assets indicate the investments in gross fixed assets minus accumulated depreciation. The investment in working capital represents the excess of current assets over current liabilities. The capital employed is also represented by the sum total of investments arising out of equity, long-term debts and internal resources.

Table 3 represents the investments by way of net fixed assets and working capital Such investments are financed by debt, equity and internal funds. The capital employed was Rs. 73300 crore in 1991. It increased to Rs. 179597 crore in 2002-03. The CAGR for capital employed was 6.74 per cent during the period under reference. The capital employed figure was about 50 per cent of the total investment pointing to the fact that the SLPEs system was not organic and required artificial respiration from time to time. The states where this phenomenon had a forceful presence included Assam, Delhi, Goa, Gujarat, Haryana, Himachal Pradesh, Karnataka, Kerala,

Maharashtra, Orissa, Punjab, Tamil Nadu, Uttar Pradesh and West Bengal. Rajasthan turned-out to be an exception indicating the appreciation for viable and self liquidating project management as the strength of the top management of the SLPEs and the policy makers in the State Government.

Chart 3: All States Capital Employed

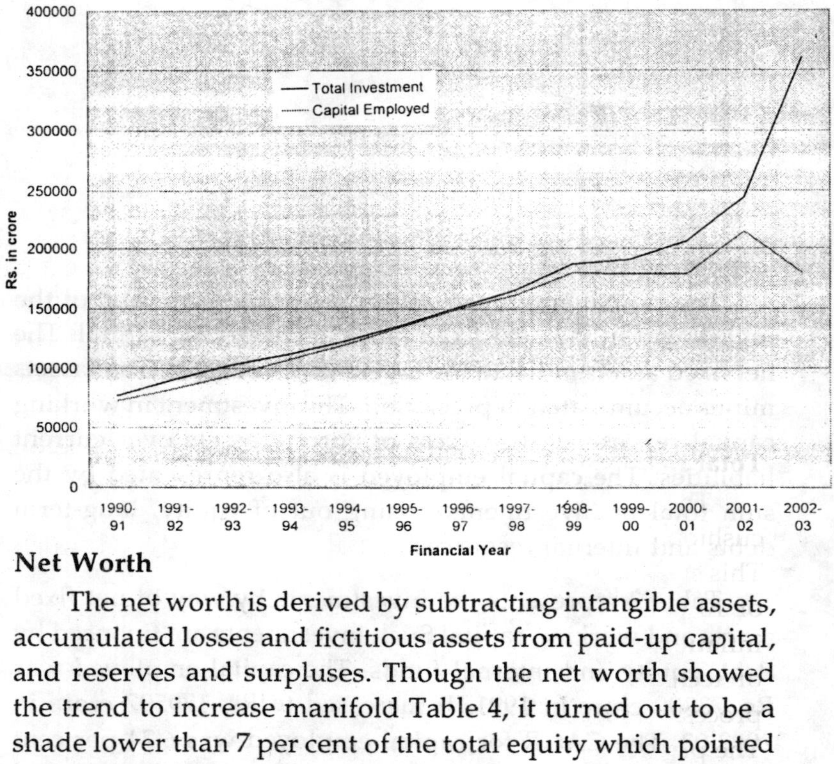

Net Worth

The net worth is derived by subtracting intangible assets, accumulated losses and fictitious assets from paid-up capital, and reserves and surpluses. Though the net worth showed the trend to increase manifold Table 4, it turned out to be a shade lower than 7 per cent of the total equity which pointed to a negligible growth in net worth and erosion of shareholders' basic capital in terms of real investment prices appearing to be a great cause of concern. The equity erosion occurred in Assam, Delhi, Goa, Kerala, Maharashtra, Mizoram, Meghalaya, Nagaland, Pondicherry, Sikkim, Tripura, Uttar Pradesh, and West Bengal. These were precisely the states where the subsidies accounted for major portion of the losses incurred.

Chart 4: All States: Total Revenue Earned

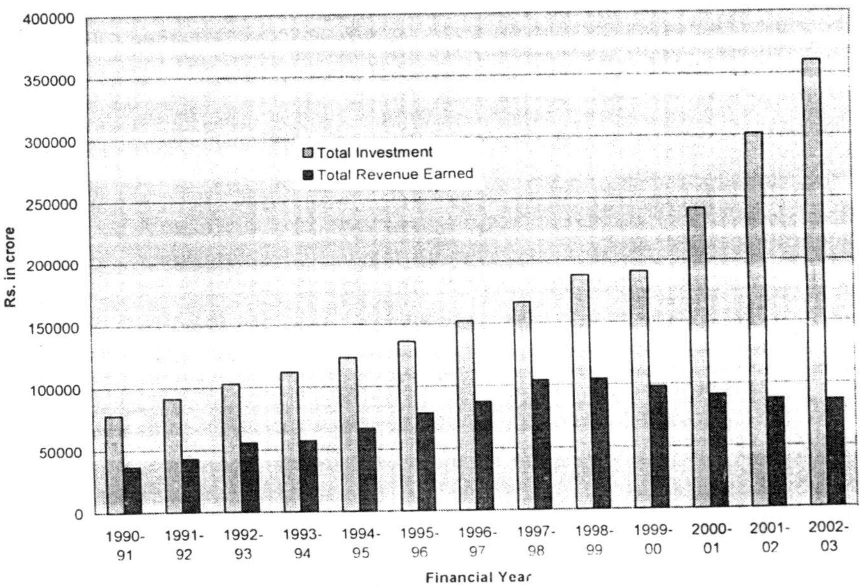

Total Revenue

This represents the top line of an enterprise. This provides cushion against contingencies and the cover to meet expenses. This should grow at least at a compound annual growth rate of 10 per cent to set off the loss caused by the real rate of inflation and meet the challenges of productivity arising out of technological advances and reorganization of business processes. This should be at least three times of the investment. The private sector multiple is five times. The multiple in the case of private sector enterprises abroad is eight times. The CAGR for total revenue for the period 1990-91 to 2002-03 was 6.93 per cent. Table 5 shows that total revenues turned out to be a discouraging figure of about 40.6 per cent of the total investment in 1990-91 and 25.00 per cent in 2002-03. The total revenue comprised the income from mainstream operations and other yields. The total revenue scenario tells many untold facts concerning lack of marketing drive, quality consciousness and soft targeting. The states which earned more than average on a rupee of investment were only handful. In 2002-03, such states included Gujarat, Madhya Pradesh, and Tamil Nadu . All the states in the country faced the challenge of unlocking the vast untapped value in the SLPEs.

Net Profits after Tax

The net profit after tax comprises a profits net of all expenses, interest and taxes. They determine the scope for and extent of allocations to reserves, dividends and surpluses. Net profit after tax is the be all and end all of all businesses. It is not only that top line is important for a business but it is also essential to ensure that the bottom line is positive. Net profit making helps in updating the technology, contribute to an organic growth and provide a unified direction. It adds to building up reserves and surpluses and higher earnings per share. Net profit making is the core element of corporatisation which takes place through the concept of equity participation, limited liability, setting up the strategic business units and practicing responsibility accounting. The operationalisation of these concepts create a harmonious internal environment where the different units/ product groups and services could compete with one another to improve their efficiency. Profitability strikes an optimum tradeoff between the demand side factors (revenues) and the supply side factors (costs) in a competitive regime. The net profits should at least be equivalent to prime lending rate or 10 per cent of the revenues earned which is the benchmark prescribed in financial management. Table 6 shows that the Net profits for all the states taken together for the various years of the study excepting 1994-95 and 1995-96 were negative. On an average, net profits for all the states taken together of the revenues earned were -2.7 per cent in 1990-91 shooting up to

-8.0 per cent in 2002-03. Delhi, Gujarat, Haryana, Kerala, Maharashtra, Punjab, Uttar Pradesh and West Bengal have been major net loss earners during 2002-03. The net losses incurred by these states not only wiped out the total profits of the profit making states but also were responsible for the phenomenon of loss making.

Accumulated Losses

The story of the SLPEs is one of accumulating losses and creating a huge pile in this regard. The accumulated losses of the SLPEs almost doubled from Rs. 10099 crore in 1991-92 to Rs. 21570 crore in 2002-03. Table 7 shows that the loss leaders comprised Andhra Pradesh, Arunachal Pradesh, Assam, Bihar, Delhi, Goa, Gujarat, Kerala, Jammu and Kashmir, Karnataka, Orissa, Pondicherry, Sikkim, Tamil Nadu, Uttar Pradesh and

Chart 5: All States: Debt Equity Ratio

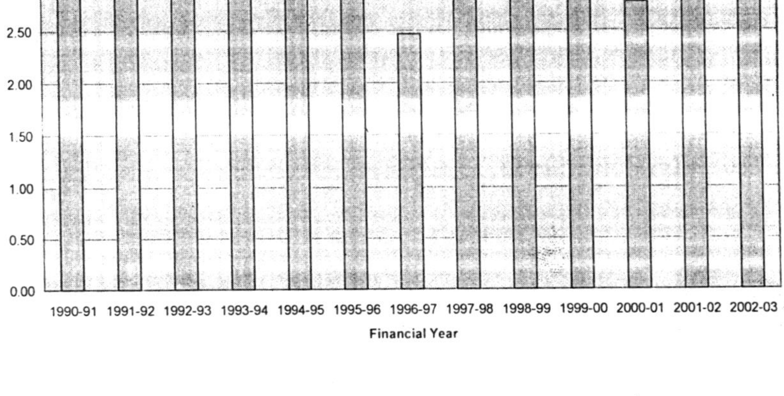

West Bengal. One of the reasons for the accumulated losses was an uncongenial debt equity ratio which was 4.27 for all the states taken together in 1990-1991 decling gradually to 2.84:1 in 2000-03 resulting in no favorable consequence as most of the states had SLPEs incurring either cash losses or losses before interest and taxes.

Total Impact on State Finances (TISF)

The financial performance of the SLPEs has a great bearing on the fiscal health of the state governments. This impact could be explained in terms of two measures. The Total Impact on the State Finance (TISF) could be shown in terms of annual outflows (sum of outflows resulting from change in state equity and debt and state subsidy and grants to SLPEs) plus the opportunity cost of investments in the SLPEs. The Gross Fiscal Impact on State Finances (GFISF) is another measure which is computed by added the sum total impact on state finances and value of guarantees outstanding given by the state SLPEs. Table 8 shows the TISF as a percentage of Tax Revenue of all the states.

TABLE 8

Fiscal Impact : All States

(in percentages)

Year	*TISF / TRS*	*GFISF/ TRS*
1996-97	35.76	115.54
1997-98	37.45	113.50
1998-99	38.19	114.48
1999-00	14.81	107.41
2000-01	30.20	129.97
2001-02	30.91	137.42
Average	31.22	119.72

Chart 1 presents the ratio of TISF to states' own tax

revenue and Chart 2 presents the ratio of GSISF to states' own tax revenue. Both the charts very clearly show the adverse impact of the non-viable working of the SLPEs on the state finances in India and hint at the possibility of a significant turnaround through the restructuring of the SLPEs.

Chart 6: TISF as a Percentage of States Own Tax Revenues (1997-2002)

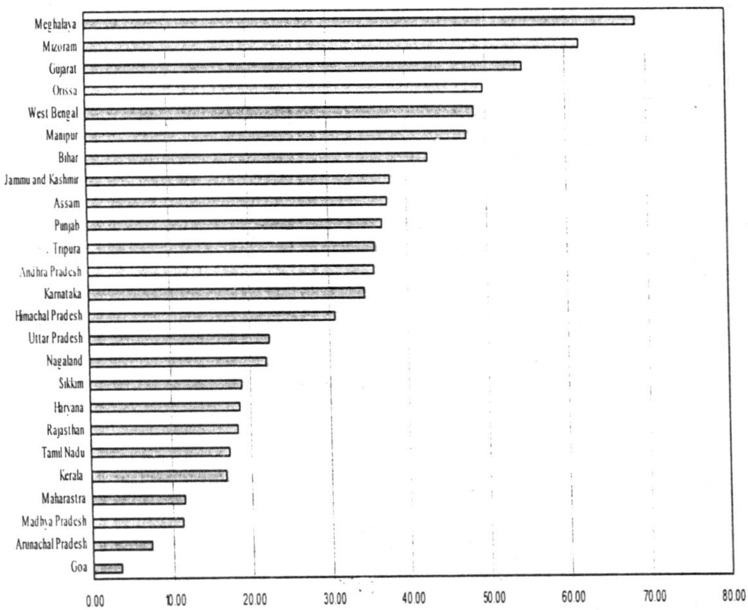

Chart 7: GFISF a Percentage of States Own Tax Revenues (1997-2002)

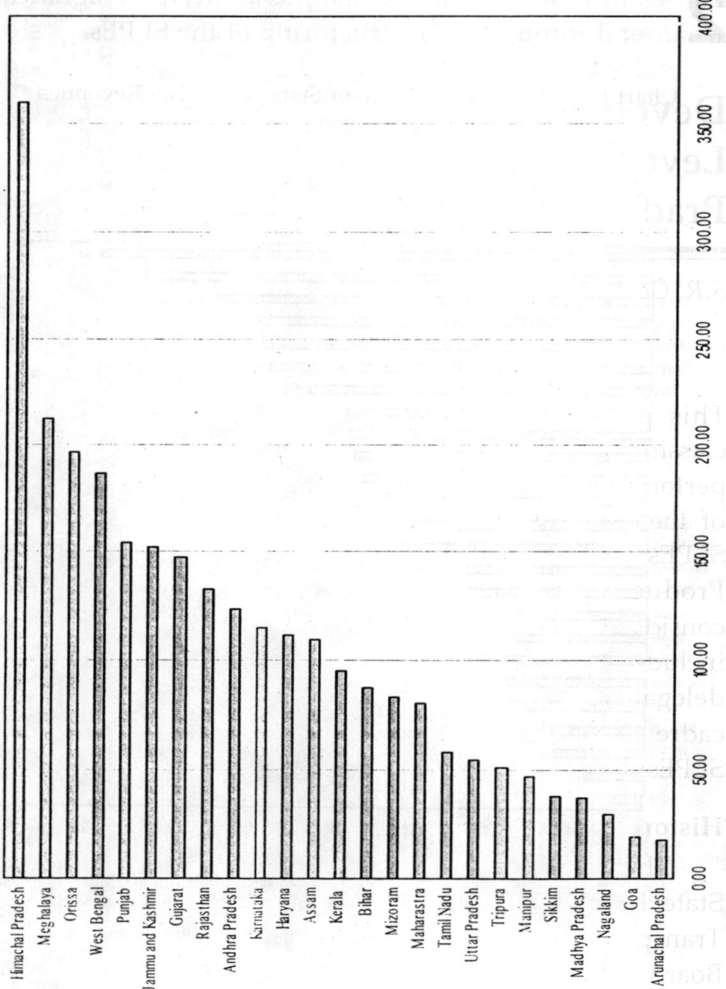

2

Development and Performance of State Level Public Enterprises in Andhra Pradesh

*S.R. Govindarajan**

This paper discusses the origin, objectives, economic classification, organizational structure, management and the performance of State Level Public Enterprises in A.P. Some of the important issues pertaining to the management of SLPEs in the state namely the role of Managing Directors, Productivity and Technological upgradation have been considered. The major recommendations made in the paper include greater operational autonomy for the SLPEs, and for delegation of investment power, institution of a common cadre and improved interface between the government and SLPEs.

Historical Development and Achievements

The Government of Andhra Pradesh have promoted 60 State Level Public Enterprises, including A.P. State Road Transport Corporation and Andhra Pradesh State Electricity Board. The identification of 'Public Enterprises' in the State of Andhra Pradesh includes registered companies, large-scale

* Director General, Public Enterprises Management Board, and Ex-Officio Secretary to Government of Andhra Pradesh, Hyderabad.

Cooperative Societies and other autonomous agencies. In fact, Co-operative Sugar factories and Co-operative Spinning Mills are also treated as State Level Public Enterprises for certain purposes, though they have their own federation and separate commissionerate. The above 60 Public Enterprises do not include Sugar Factories and Spinning Mills.

The origin of state undertakings in the State of Andhra Pradesh goes deep into the history, even to the period prior to the formation of Andhra Pradesh. Erstwhile Nizam of Hyderabad gave a spurt to industrialisation in his State by generously investing in industrial enterprises from a pool of funds, specially created for this purpose and also by promoting other enterprises actively.

Many of these enterprises started during his time are still in existence like HYDERABAD ALLWYN, HYDERABAD CHEMICALS & FERTILIZERS, REPUBLIC FORGE CO., etc. Some of them were taken over by the Nizam after the first promoter could not successfully complete the project. The management of these enterprises was first entrusted to a managing agency and subsequently it was taken over by the Government.

A significant thrust was given to the starting of Public Enterprises after Independence and after the formation of State of Andhra Pradesh and then Andhra Pradesh under the National Policy Guidelines, about 25 years back, the Andhra Pradesh Industrial Development Corporation, Andhra Pradesh State Finance Corporation and Andhra Pradesh Small Scale Industrial Development Corporation were started along the pattern of other States. Subsequently, other enterprises like State level Apex Weavers Cooperative Society (APCO), Dairy Development Corporation, (not APDDCF) , Agro Industries Development Corporation, Seeds Development Corporation, Warehousing Corporation, MARKFED, Civil Supplies

Corporation etc. were started. While many of the above enterprises were similar to the attempts elsewhere, certain innovative and original steps to be taken in the State of Andhra Pradesh should be highlighted. These include starting of Andhra Pradesh Non-Resident Indian Corporation (ANRICH), Andhra Pradesh Heavy Machinery Engineering Limited, Andhra Pradesh Industrial Infrastructure Corporation, Andhra Pradesh Minorities Finance Corporation, Andhra Pradesh Scooters, Federation of Sericulture Cooperative Societies (SERIFED), Federation of Cooperative Rice Mills (RICEFED), Rural Irrigation Corporation, State Irrigation Development Corporation, Police Housing Corporation, Weaker .Section Housing Corporation, Andhra ,Pradesh Technology Services Corporation, Andhra Pradesh Beverages Corporation and Shore Area'' Development Authority. These enterprises have been started with a, specific objective in view and in response to the demand from the public. Andhra Pradesh Heavy Machinery Engineering Limited is perhaps the only one of its kind, where a State Level Public Enterprise has been started in response to public initiative and cooperation. The people of Krishna District came forward and contributed to the share capital in a very large number with a view to starting an engineering unit for the manufacture of leather machinery textile machinery heavy machinery etc., in the industrially backward area. Since the investment is heavy in nature the Government took note of the initiative and started the public enterprises by contributing major part of the equity.

Realising the potential for sericulture especially in the tribal areas and dry-belt areas the Federation of Sericulture Cooperative Societies has been started to give necessary technical input and marketing thrust. Similarly Police Housing Corporation has been created for the construction of Police Station Buildings and quarters for policemen in a big way. This example has now been adopted by a number of other States.

Under weaker sections, housing the achievement of Andhra Pradesh is an enviable one. More than 1 lakh houses are being constructed every year through the weaker section housing corporation. Though Andhra Pradesh is surplus in power, the need for developing non-conventional energy and for channelising the promotional efforts to tap non-conventional Energy resources and encouraging individual and community units has been realised and the non-conventional Energy Development Corporation has been organised.

These examples can be multiplied. However the basic theme is that the Government is opening up new directions and areas for the State Level Public Enterprises. Keeping in view the changing demands and the political and social priorities. All the steps are innovative and highlight the shift in the strategic objectives of the State Level Public Enterprises.

Objectives of State Level Public Enterprises

As stated above many specific enterprises have been started with well-laid-down objectives. An attempt has been made to evolve overall strategic objectives for all the enterprises and also specific objectives for each enterprise. Though, the constitution of the Public Enterprises, through its memorandum of association, spells out large, main, immediate and desirable objectives. It is necessary to lay down the immediate and priority objectives. For this purpose the State Level Enterprises have been divided into a matrix format of 4 categories as under:

1. Commercial
2. Competitive enterprises
3. Commercial
4. Monopoly enterprises
5. Non-commercial

6. Non-competitive enterprises
7. Non-commercial competitive enterprises.

Non-Commercial, Competitive Enterprises are rare. In the State of Andhra Pradesh, it has been very clearly laid down as the objective for all the State Level Public Enterprises that they should function profitably, balancing their resources and expenditure, taking care of their regular maintenance and even growth. That means each enterprise should plan its expenditure within its resources of income. If the Government desires any Public Enterprise to subsidise its services or products, to the extent of the subsidy element the enterprise will be compensated if it could not find the amount of subsidy from its other resources. For the competitive commercial enterprises, the objective is that they should give return on investment on par with private sector units in the same line. This applies to enterprises like Hyderabad Allwyn.

The commercial, Non-competitive Enterprises operate in an atmosphere of monopoly or administered price. APSRTC and APSES and Units like them fall under this category. For them, the objective is controlling of cost and rendering of service at/the lowest cost. Price fixation is done keeping in view their desirable cost structure and over and above that giving a small margin for the enterprises to survive and grow. This policy has been adopted for Andhra Pradesh Beverages Corporation which is bottling and supplying country liquor to the Government of Andhra Pradesh.

In the case of Non-Commercial Enterprises profit is not the motive. For them, the cost of services rendered by them should be within limits. They are paid the estimated cost of service, with some margin over and above it and their performance is judged with reference to this.

For the first 'time the draft strategic guidelines has been

prepared for all the State Level Public Enterprises. This is in the process of being finalised after interaction with a wide range of persons and agencies.

The Public Enterprises are also divided under 4 categories based on these activities viz., (1) Production Enterprises (2) Trading Enterprises (3) Welfare Enterprises (4) Promotional and Development Enterprises. Naturally, the objectives for the' enterprises under these 4 categories will vary and shall be distinguished. Production Enterprises are mostly in the commercial sector and for them capacity utilisation and achievement of financial objectives are important.

Trading Enterprises either supply essential commodities at provide marketing services to the other units. Their objective should be to function efficiently, identify markets to give feedback to the manufacturing centres and also supply the commodities at the appropriate price, quality and time. They should discharge these duties with cost effectiveness, within the limits fixed.

Welfare Corporations fall into a different category; they do not have any commercial objective. That serve mostly the social purpose of assisting the weaker sections to rise above the poverty line.

For the State of Andhra Pradesh, the following corporations are recognised as welfare corporations:

1. Andhra Pradesh Housing Corporation
2. Andhra Pradesh S.C. Cooperative Finance Corporation
3. Andhra Pradesh Backward Class Finance Corporation
4. Andhra Pradesh S.T. Cooperative Finance Corporation
5. Andhra Pradesh Vikalangula Corporation
6. Girijan Cooperative Corporation.

In their cases, the effectiveness and the timeliness of the service rendered to the weaker sections is the main objective. This service should also be rendered with cost effectiveness.

The development and promotional corporations promote and help to prosper many industrial and other units, under the joint sector and assist the sector. The following corporations are recognised as promotional corporations:

1. Andhra Pradesh Industrial Development Corporation
2. Andhra Pradesh State Financial Corporation
3. Andhra Pradesh Industrial Infrastructure Corporation
4. Andhra Pradesh Small Scale Industrial Development Corporation
5. Andhra Pradesh Handicrafts Development Corporation
6. AP Electronics Development Corporation
7. AP Agro Industries Development Corporation.

Their objective is to, promote as many units as possible in the chosen field and ensure their continued prosperity and growth. As such, measurement of their achievement will be in terms of number of units promoted successfully and the employment generated, area developed and wealth created, addition to GDP etc. While rendering the service efficiently, they have also to ensure cost effectiveness.

Organisational Structure

The State Level Public Enterprises have got the following types of constitutions:

1. Registered Company
2. Cooperative Society (Apex or Unitary)
3. Society registered under the Societies Act

4. Statutory Corporation
5. Other autonomous authorities.

Out of 60 State Level Public Enterprises stated above, the classification by way of organisational structure is as under:

1. Corporate setup (Registered Companies) (38)
2. Cooperative setup (15)
3. Registered Societies (1)
4. Statutory Corporations (5)
5. Autonomous Agencies (1).

The constitution of the Public Enterprise viz., corporate set up or co-operative set up etc. is based on the needs of the organisation and the proposed activity. Naturally, the apex body of co-operative societies has got to be a co-operative federation. For this reason the D.D.C.F, which was earlier a registered company, was recently transformed into a cooperative federation.

In the recent past we were preferring a corporate setup. However, this organisation requires an annual expenditure over the year, as many returns have to be filed and records kept all under the Companies Act. We are following the logic that wherever it involves raising of institutional finance and undertaking of commercial activities and when determining the profit or loss on the working of the organisation over the period is necessary or desirable. A registered company is to be preferred.

Wherever commercial activity is not anticipated and raising of institutional finance is not of importance. A registered society or an autonomous agency through a Government order is preferred. Telugu Samacharam, Telugu Ganga and Shore Area Development Authority are autonomous units set up by an executive order.

The implication of taxation law and the need or otherwise of a legal identity should also be kept in view. From the efficiency of working the author would like to recommend a registered company for all activities as such an organisation presupposes certain discipline to be observed under the Companies Act, 1956.

Management

All the State Level Public Enterprises are given a Board of Directors and a Chief Executive for the management of the affairs of the enterprise. The State Government of Andhra Pradesh has evolved certain guidelines regarding the constitution of the Board of Directors of the Public Enterprises. According to these guidelines the maximum number of Directors on the Board of any Company or Corporation is not to exceed 12. In the case of manufacturing or commercial undertakings this number is restricted to 7.

In the constitution of the Board of Directors 1/3 of the Directors are to be drawn from Government, representing the controlling departments in Government like Finance and other departments, 1/3 of the number of Directors are to be drawn from competent professionals in the fields of financial management, production, inventory etc., and the remaining vacancies to be filled with representatives of special interests, regions or individuals, by appointment of public men from different walks of life. Each Board should have a term of two years.

The above guidelines have been drawn up after detailed consideration and deliberations. However in real practice, there is a deviation from these guidelines. While the total number of directors by and large is restricted to 12, the composition of the Board of Directors varies considerably from time to time. This appears to be inevitable because of the nature of constitution of the Board of Directors by the Government.

Chairmen and The Chief Executive

We have tried to evolve certain guidelines regarding the appointment of Chairmen of Board of Directors. The general approach or thinking is that for corporations having close interaction with the public, where feedback from the public is necessary and where public representatives will be of great assistance, the Chairman of the Board of Directors could be a man from public life. However, in practice such a rigid classification or approach is not found to be workable. The Government of Andhra Pradesh have tried and are continuing to try, professionals, technocrats, civil servants, working or retired and public men as Chairmen of Board of Directors. From the experience so far there is nothing to indicate that there could be uniform guidelines, which could be followed profitably.

From the list of Chairmen and Board of Directors it may be seen that out of 44 enterprises in list, Chairmen for IS Corporations are serving or retired civil servants. Chairmen of 9 corporations are professionals or technocrats. The remaining are from public life. However, this ratio is changing from time to time.

Out of the above 44 enterprises, the position of Chief Executive is held by regular Government officers in 33 undertakings; for the remaining 11, Chief Executives have been selected from inside the Corporation or from the open market.

The Government of Andhra Pradesh have drawn up elaborate guidelines regarding the functions of the Chairman of the Board of Directors, his perks and other claims. Flexibility is given to the Chairman of the Board of Directors to spend as much time as he could spare and feel like spending on the management of the Public Enterprises.

We have suggested that, over and above provisions

regarding the powers of the Chairman of the Board of Directors, Directors and the Board of Directors under the Companies Act ,.or the other statutes, every company may constitute sub-committees to be presided over by the Chairman, for major sections of management like purchases, recruitment, promotions, corporate plan etc.

Depending upon the turnover of the respective corporations the Board of Directors may also delegate powers to the Managing Directors to sanction schemes etc. In addition separately. We have also recommended a model scheme of delegation.

As per these guidelines the Chairman shall have power to send for any information from the Managing" Director from time to time without detriment to the day-to-day functioning of the Managing Director. However the Managing Director shall be responsible for the implementation of all the resolutions passed by the Board of Directors. To this extent the Chairman shall have supervisory control over the Managing Director.

In modification of the earlier guidelines the tenure of the Chairman of the Board of Directors has been fixed now as one year. It has also been prescribed that not less than 50% of the Board of Directors in any Board shall consist of non-officials. The above guidelines while to some extent have created a threetier set up in the Corporation's management viz., Board of Directors, Committee of Directors and the Managing Director, number of issues have to be sorted out and clarified from time to time involving the Chairman and the Managing Director. We are actively engaged in preparing detailed guidelines for this purpose.

The tenure of the Board of Directors has been restricted to one year in the State of Andhra Pradesh with the idea of evaluating the performance of the members of the Board and then granting extension in deserving cases. While this has worked to fix answerability on the members of the Board of Directors there is the other argument that one year is too short a period. Moreover with one year tenure the Board is not likely to consider any long-term proposal with gestation period of more than one year.

The Board of Directors of all the Public Enterprises are meeting regularly. The State Government has advised that for each meeting of the Board of Directors certain items like performance during the last intervening period should be placed before the Board. This way it has been made almost compulsory to review the performance of the Enterprise at every Board meeting.

Under these guidelines amongst other things it has been suggested that the Agenda items of any meeting of the Board of any Public Enterprise shall consist of the following: (1) Minutes of the previous meeting of the Board of Directors; (2) Leave of Absence; (3) Any changes in the Board arising as a result of Government nominations or nominations by institutions; (4) Performance of the Public Enterprise in terms of physical targets during period between last meeting and present one; under this item the Managing Director should indicate briefly what has been the target set and what has been the achievement; (5) Progress in marketing the products of the Corporation; (6) Financial position of the company and the requirement of money; (7) Staff position (8) Progress in respect of new projects and (9) Any general and special instructions from the Government or financial institutions, received since the last meeting.

Subsequently, it has also been suggested that compliance with statutory requirement should also be reported in the Agenda items of the Board of Directors. By and large these guidelines have helped the Board to consider all the important and relevant matters, assess the working of the enterprises without fault.

Nominee Directors

The Board of Directors of all the Public Enterprises, invariably, have nominee directors of the Government. They are ex-officio members of the Board. Normally, one representative each from the Finance Department and the Administrative Department is nominated to these Boards. Government have taken a policy decision that as far as possible officers below the rank of secretaries to .Government will be nominated to the Board. The exception is only in the case of corporations like SFC, IDC, etc.

Detailed guidelines have been issued regarding the functions of the nominee directors. (G.O.Ms.No.63, dated 2-2-84, page 96 of Compendium of Guidelines Vol. I).

Under these guidelines it has been suggested that the nominee Directors should ensure that, amongst others, the following matters are included in the Agenda for every Board meeting. It has also been suggested that the nominee directors should ensure that the corporate plan is prepared for the organisation. Subsequently, it has also been prescribed that nominee directors shall ensure compliance with all statutory provisions of the Public Enterprises.

In order to have regular feedback for the Administration Department and the Government from the nominee directors, a report has been prescribed to be given by every nominee director, after every Board meeting. In this regard, the experiment of IDBI in having whole time, trained, professionals nominee directors is also worth mentioning. Government of Andhra Pradesh is examining carefully various suggestions for making nominee Directors effective in their functions.

The feedback report, if furnished regularly, will be given

necessary details in brief, regarding functioning of the enterprise, profitability or otherwise, payments made, industrial relations, compliance with statutory requirements, progress of projects, etc. However, this may require further training for the nominee directors and prescription of regular reporting systems in the enterprises.

Human Resources Management

One of the main objectives for the State Level Public Enterprise is to ensure total human resources development in the individual enterprises. This includes man-power planning, compensation, continued learning, organisational structure, selection, training, performance appraisal, promotion etc.

The ill of surplus man-power is Public Enterprises could be avoided if proper corporate plans are prepared and commensurate with them man-power requirements are also estimated. A beginning has been made in this direction in the State of Andhra Pradesh. Keeping in view the necessary flexibility and autonomy for the enterprises management and the need for avoiding indiscriminate appointment of staff, it has been prescribed that before the beginning of every year the enterprise will prepare its detailed action programme, keeping in view the priorities set by the Government and the financial limitations. Along with this action programme, the man-power requirements for achieving this action programme should also be estimated. Thereafter, any deficiency in man-power, category wise, keeping in view the existing strength, future requirements and the future wastages is to be estimated. This man power got approved by the Government along with action Programme this way rearly man power planning is being achieved. However, for better results, it is necessary that long range man power planning should also be undertaken.

In the selection of requisite personnel, maximum autonomy is given to the enterprises. Barring the Chief Executives and Board level positions, for all the other positions the enterprises call for applications and take up the recruitment. Upto posts carrying Rs. 1500 basic pay, the enterprise makes the selection without any representative from outside. However, for the posts carrying basic pay of Rs. 1500/- to Rs. 2000 in the selection committee of the enterprises a representative of the DG PEMB is nominated. Normally he is an expert member. For the posts carrying more than Rs. 2000 basic pay, selection committee is constituted with the Chief Executive of the organisation, D.G., PEMB and other outside experts as members along with the Chairman of the Board of Directors of the organisation. For the level of Chief Executives and Board level positions, a high level selection committee is constituted with the Secretary as the Chairman, Secretary of the concerned Administrative Department, D.G., PEMB, Chairman of the Board of Directors, Chief Executive and the expert members as members of the Committee. This procedure has ensured impartiality and uniformity, in the selection of executives for the State Level Enterprises.

Public Enterprises Personnel Board

A proposal for setting up a state level Public Enterprises Personnel Board (PEMB) for taking up overall Man Power Planning and Human Resources Development in all the State Level Public Enterprises, with full autonomy to recruit senior and Board Level Executives, have been approved by the Government of Andhra Pradesh.

Tenure, Compensation and Training

The above system of recruitment has ensured impartiality and selection of qualified candidates for the State Level Public Enterprises. It has contributed to the improvement in their working. In the matter of emoluments for various posts,

Government of Andhra Pradesh have taken number of progressive steps. They have de-linked the scales of pay of the Executives of State Level Public Enterprises from those in the Government, except for those who go on deputation. Keeping in view the requirement of the post, the responsibility, qualifications prescribed and the offer from competitors, scales of pay have been fixed for various senior levels in the various public enterprises. Rigid uniformity is not enforced. The only aim is to obtain the services of competent executives.

There is also a uniform policy of recruiting professional executives from the market and keeping to the minimum and, if possible, totally eliminate deputationists, in positions other than the Chief Executives and thereby professionalise management of State Level Public Enterprises fully. Wherever possible, the executives are taken on a contract tenure of 3 years. This is to ensure proper performance and answerability. Training of the top and middle-level managers of Public Enterprises is being given maximum importance. The PEMB is conducting monthly management development programme for the senior executives every month. These programmes are conducted keeping in view the felt need for additional skills or training in the Public Enterprises, as suggested by the Chief Executives or as diagnosed after reviewing their performance. They are conducted with expert faculty from among the well-known training institutions like Administrative Staff College of India (ASCI), Institute of Public Enterprise (IPE), Andhra Pradesh Productivity Council (APPC), institute of Financial Management and Research (IFMR) etc. The fact that many of these training institutions located in Hyderabad is a great advantage, which is being made use of. These executive training programmes have been designed with a lot of innovations. All programmes invariably include, besides theoretical and academic input, cases from the local State Level Public Enterprises for discussions and practical talks by Managers and Chief Executives of our own Public Enterprises which have also been included besides an exercise on the Computers.

Reading material is prepared carefully along with standard books of reference, which are supplied to all the participants. These programmes are very much appreciated and have contributed to the improvement on the performance of the Public Enterprises. Besides training the executives as above, the need for having systematic training programmes for supervisors, staff and workers has also been recognised. Large-scale Public Enterprises have been encouraged to start their own training institutes and take up training programmes. APCO and a few other institutions have made a beginning in this way. An attempt is also being made to identify the training needs systematically. All the public Enterprises have been addressed to categorise their skill requirements and then identify the present level of skills and deficiency, if any. At a later date it will be consolidated and skill-wise training modules will be prepared and training programmes will be undertaken in the individual enterprises for the staff and workers also.

Performance Evaluation

Internal performance evaluation of the Managers and Executives of the Public Enterprises has to be modernised. So far, the system of evaluation is along conventional lines of annual reporting. A system of Management Accounting, along with organising the enterprises into cost-profit centres, is necessary.

At the Government level, evaluate the performance of the Public Enterprises has been given serious attention. The result of our experience is the realisation that their could be no single criteria or formula for evaluating the performance of all the Public Enterprises, as a whole. In order to have a comparative idea of the performance of the various public enterprises the Government of Andhra Pradesh has evolved Public Enterprises Performance Index.

As discussed above, the various public enterprises could be classified under Commercial and Non-Commercial undertaking which will have distinct and separate financial and non-financial targets. The performance appraisal pre-supposes clear determination and understanding of the corporate objectives strategy to be adopted, prioritisation of the objectives, output measurement parameters, impartial authority for the fixation of targets and measurement of performance and comparison of performance with the targets. In the absence of these, any exercise undertaken in performance appraisal for all the corporations, is likely to be unsatisfactory and counter-productive through the Public Enterprises Management Board (PEMB), Key Result Areas for each Enterprise, keeping in view their corporate objectives and prescribed strategy. For these Key Result Areas, which may vary from 3 to 7 for each enterprise, targets are set in physical and financial terms, for every year, in the beginning of the year itself. Thereafter, the performance of the enterprise is measured against these targets. Weightage is given to the various Key Result Areas, depending on the system of prioritisatio which may vary from time to time. One of the Key result Areas is the financial results or profit earned, target for which will be different for commercial and non-commercial undertakings.

Achievement of the targets under the Key Result Areas alone may not be indicating the efficiency of performance. For this purpose, for the various Key Result Areas, productivity indicators have also been identified. These Productivity indicators are Factor Productivity indicators and total productivity indicators; they may be the percentage cost of raw material in total cost of production, Administration expenses as a percentage of income, capital turnover capacity utilisation, working capital turnover, number of days sales in debtors, return on investment, return on capital utilisation, working capital turnover, number of days sales in debtors, return on investment, return on capital employed, profit on sales, cost of servicing 1000 beneficiaries, cost of distribution of one crore of loan etc. These indicators are fixed for each year and the actual achievements are judged against these indicators. Weightages are given for each indicator, keeping in view their importance' for the public enterprise. While the above Key Result Areas and Productivity indicators may suffice to judge the performance in the course of one year, it may not take into consideration the continued good performance of the organisation or may not guarantee good performance beyond the period of appraisal. For this purpose, the organisation should have certain, long-range objectives and measures, like corporate planning, modernisation technology, introduction of computers, man-power planning etc. These can be called Management Systems which are very necessary for the survival and future growth of the organisation. The appropriate systems to be introduced will vary from time to time and from organisation to, organisation and is entirely dependent upon the felt needs. In the total performance appraisal, the introduction and functioning of the systems should be given weightage.

Incorporation of the various above performance parameters, along with human resources development and other routine functions a composite, multi-variant performance index is being prepared for every enterprise, for every quarter. The performance of the enterprises, over the year, is ranked. The Government of Andhra Pradesh have also announced an award scheme for the best performing enterprise.

Internal Management

The State Level Public Enterprises have been given

autonomy to evolve appropriate internal management systems like Information Systems, Budget and Budgetary Control, Internal Audit etc. However, an overview of the practice obtaining in the enterprises gives one the feeling that in the absence of proper guidance, assistance and control, these management systems have become a casualty. As such, Government of Andhra Pradesh through 'Public Enterprises Management Board' (PEMB) have taken up development of appropriate Management and Control Systems in the State Level Public Enterprises. As a first step, services have been offered to the various enterprises for developing Corporate plan, Internal Audit, Management Information System and Organisation structure and Man power planning. Each enterprise could pick and choose whatever it needs most.

Tata Consultancy Services (TCS) have been engaged for designing proper Management Information Systems, which could be computerised, in 10 selected Public Enterprises. These Enterprises are varied in nature like RFC, B.C. Welfare Cooperate Finance Corporation, SSIDC, etc. TCS have held detailed discussions with the D.G., PEMB and the Executives of the respective enterprises, identified their corporate objectives, responsibility centres and appropriate reporting systems. It is in final shape and will be implemented in the near future.

We have also taken up introduction of modern internal auditing in selected enterprises. This concept of internal auditing is far different from what is presently obtaining, namely, passing of bills and checking of vouchers.

The main thrust of this modern internal auditing is efficiency auditing or operations auditing or performance auditing. It is for determining the adequacy and efficiency or otherwise of the internal control systems, not only on financial transactions but also all operations of the organisations. We have prepared a general manual which will give the guidelines for all the Public Enterprises to introduce the state of art internal auditing. For selected enterprises, we have also prepared a detailed manual (Part-II) giving the questionnaire approach for appraising their various operations. We have conducted training programmes for the senior executives in the introduction of modern internal auditing. We have also conducted continuing Education Programme through Jawaharlal Nehru Technological University, Hyderabad on Internal Auditing. Enterprises like Agro Industries Development Corporation, Irrigation Development Corporation etc. have been selected for this purpose. It is hoped that over a period of time the benefit of internal auditing will be seen in improved performance.

Steps have been taken to streamline the budgeting process. Two workshops have been conducted on modern concepts of Budget and Budgetary control. Focus is upon performance Budgeting, Zero Base Budgeting, and Flexible Budgeting. A lot more will have to be done with the modernisation of Office Administration, upgradation of technology and information system. It is in this direction that our future efforts will be concentrated.

Technical Areas

Technical areas like production, marketing and financial management, require more attention in all the Public Enterprises. Production process in many Public Enterprises has to be urgently modernised to improve productivity. Especially units in the competitive sector find themselves unable to compete with private units, which have improved quality of the product and the technology of the process and with improved productivity they are able to dominate the market. A typical example is a forging unit, which, though it was once working very profitably over a period of about a decade, did not progress much in the direction of improving man productivity or raw material productivity and consequently is now facing severe competition and heavy losses.

There is no organised central guidance in this matter. Similarly, in marketing also public enterprises are found to be very much lacking, especially if they are in a competitive environment. Cash Management is another area which will require vast improvement and attention.

Control System

The State Level Public Enterprises fall under the control of various Administrative Departments of Government. Through these departments they are subjected to the control of the committee on Public Undertakings. Public Accounts Committee, Consulative Committee for Finance and the State Legislature. Though the concerned Secretary to the Government normally answers these committees the involvement of the Public Enterprises management cannot be reduced. The relationship between the State Legislature, Legislative Committees, The Administrative Department and the Public Enterprises is practically the same as is obtaining for Central undertakings; any change in this regard only at the State Level is not possible.

However, in order to give full autonomy to the State Level Public Enterprises and assist them in having clear goals and strategy for achieving- them, without the need for day-to-day interference and also in order t~ have a professional policy making group to guide the public enterprises as well as the State Government, the Government of Andhra Pradesh have created Public Enterprises Management Board (PEMB). This is a semi-official and semi-professional Autonomous board. The Chairmanship of the Board rests with the Chief Secretary to Government and the Industries and Finance Secretaries to the Government. D.G., PEMB and E.O Secretary to Government are the full time members of the Board in the Ex-officio capacity.

Besides the above official members, four professional experts are being nominated to the Board from time to time; as expert members. Presently these four professional are one cost Accountant, one Chartered. One Banker and one Financial Expert. It is also proposed to nominate experts from Marketing and Personnel Management fields.

The main functions of the PEMB can be listed out as under:

- To serve as a central forum of reference and consultation for the departments, on matters of general interest to the Public Enterprises, like organization, Management Methods, Personnel Management, Financial Management, Training Programmes, etc.
- To assist the Government in laying down general principles, procedures and methodologies regarding the matters connected with Public Enterprises with a view to improve their performance and to bring about a degree of comparability and measure of uniformity in pay scales perquisites service matters, reporting-etc.
- To assist the concerned administrative departments and the Government in monitoring the performance of Public Enterprises.
- To prepare periodic evaluation reports on the performance of Public Enterprises.
- To assist the departments in determining appropriate budgetary support for the Public Enterprises.
- o effect necessary coordination between the enterprises and the Government.

- To assist the Public Enterprises in evolving appropriate long-range plans.
- To take up periodic review of the performance of the undertakings.
- To appraise the investment proposals of the Public Enterprises and advise the Government as well as the Public Enterprises.

It may be seen that the PEMB is an advisory body, professional in nature and is not a regulatory or administrative body. Over a period of 5 years PEMB has evolved a system of working by which it makes its expert advise available to the Administrative Departments as well as Public Enterprises. Because of the nature of the constitution of PEMB and the contents of the advice, they are invariably accepted by the Government. However, formal acceptance from the Government is still necessary.

Over a period, D.G., PEMB has organised the following activities.

- Assisting the Government in finalising the annual action programme and in setting up targets under KRAs and Productivity Indicators for each enterprise in the beginning of the Year. For this purpose a Secretaries Committee has been constituted and the Public Enterprises are ready with all the details of the entire annual action programme, budgetary support and the fixation of targets are completed by the first of April itself. This is no mean achievement.
- Reviewing the performance of Public Enterprises once in a quarter with reference to the various targets and identifying the problem areas and rendering necessary assistance.
- For undertaking these activities the Secretariat of the

PEMB consists of whole time D.G., PEMB and three professional adviser in the fields of Finance, Production, and Personnel Management.

This experiment of Government of Andhra Pradesh in constituting an expert PEMB, has certainly introduced the desirable professional approach in dealing with matters concerning Public Enterprises in the Government and also in the management of Public enterprises.

Overview of the Performance of Andhra Pradesh SLPEs

Institute of Public Enterprise has prepared an analytical study of the performance and financial pattern of selected SLPEs for the years 1981-82 to 1983-84. For subsequent years D.G., PEMB has prepared a detailed report on the performance of these' enterprises including their financial data.

The report of the Institute of Public Enterprise provided data on investment in AP SLPEs. From the analysis contains in this report it is seen that Equity in the SLPEs, numbering 25, was in the range of 30 to 35% and long time loans, 67 to 69% of the total investments. It may be seen that this is comparable with the position obtaining in the private sector.

During the period 1981-83 to 1983-84, income of the 25 selected Public Enterprises increased from Rs. 595 crores to 923 crores. The expenditure during the same period followed suit. It increased from Rs. 537 crores to Rs. 891 crores. It may be noted that positive contribution, by way of excess of income over expenditure during this period increased significantly.

It may be seen from these figures that the gross profit, which was 57.85 crores during 1981-82, got reduced to Rs. 38.99 crores in 1983-84 and profit before tax was a net loss of Rs. 50.61 crores. The contribution to the exchequer by the selected 25 State Level Public Enterprises, during these 3 years, was of the order of Rs. 45.94 crores in 1981-82, which increased to Rs. 67 crores in 83-84.

During this year they incurred a net loss of Rs. 47.24 crores, which was less than the loss incurred 3 1983-84.

The performance of these enterprises during 1985-86 is a landmark. During this year 42 public enterprises gave a net profit of Rs. 74.43 crores. During this year they also increased their turnover by more than 30% and the number of loss-making enterprises came down from 24 to 17.

The same upward trend continued in 1986-87 also. In this year too these enterprises made a net profit of about Rs. 70 crores, which worked out to return of more than 7% on the capital invested by the Government.

All in all, it has to be said that the various steps discussed above and taken so far, have transformed the working of the State Level 'Public Enterprises and put them on a firm footing.

Issues for Discussion

Productivity: The concept of productivity in Public Enterprises has to take deep root. Each Enterprise should have its own productivity target and productivity plan. Getting the commitment of all the workers for the possibility of linked promotions, revision of scales of pay, bonus and other incentives to productivity improvement needs more consideration.

Decision-making: The authority and capacity for taking appropriate decisions in the State Level Public Enterprises needs improvement. It is suggested that on all operational issues, the decisions should be entirely with the Public Enterprises management. This includes projects, selection of contractors, promotion within the organisation, etc. For this purpose, proper professional heads would be appointed. In matters involving strategy, long range targets, and corporate priorities, Government should retain the authority.

Technology: As discussed above, technology upgradation needs more attention in the Public Enterprises. Periodically, technology audit and improvement plan is recommended.

Investment decisions: Wherever a Public Enterprise could finance the investment to be made internally, probably the decision could be left to the enterprise's management upto a larger limit. However, if it involves financing by the Government, the decision will require approval by the Government

Common cadre: The possibility and desirability of creating common cadres for Public Enterprises has been discussed from time to time. Several items would have to be worked into before arriving at an acceptable decision in this matter.

Recuitment for top positions: Recruitment for top positions should be both from inside the organisation and as well as outside to get the best talent. We recommend a centralized agency like personal Board for the recruiment of top level executives.

Funding pattern: The pattern of funding for investment in Public Enterprises is not uniform or comparable between the Central and State Level undertakings. However, since the concept of Public Enterprises has been founded to top non-government resources, it will be appropriate to have a debt equity ratio similarly to private enterprises. This policy we have already adopted for Andhra Pradesh State Level Public Enterprises.

Product mix and marketing decisions: It is suggested that as regards marketing, selection of products and even pricing, full operational freedom should be given to the Public Enterprises, subject to such guidelines or limitations as

Government may choose to fix, from the social or political point of view.

Performance indicators: Proper performance indicators may be designed to reflect the achievement of the Public Enterprises both in financial and non-financial fields. We suggest an annual social cost-benefit analysis apart from the financial statements.

TABLE 2.1

Profile of SLPEs of A.P

(Rs. in. crores)

Items / *Years*	*1998-99*	*1999-00*	*2000-01*	*2001-02*	*2002-03*	*2003-04*
1. Total no. of SLPEs	41	48	51	51	49	48
2. No.of Working SLPEs	29	34	37	36	31	31
3. No.of Non-Working SLPEs	12	14	14	15	18	17
(i) Under liquidation	1	1	6	6	14	9
(ii) Under Closure		7	5	5		4
(iii) Under Merger		2	1	1		1
(iv) Others	11	4	2	3	4	3
4. Total Equity (Rs. in crore)	1850.28	3670.66	5224.74	7426.66	7328.04	7328.04
5. Total Debt (Rs. in crore)	3774.87	11289.39	12169.65	13211.63	19138.62	19138.62
6. Total Investment (Rs. in crore)	5625.15	14960.05	17394.39	20638.29	26538.41	26538.41
7. No. of Profit making enterprises	14	15	15	15	15	12
8. No. of Loss making enterprises	22	22	23	25	14	16
9. Net Profit/Loss (Rs. in crore)	52.32	79.53	235.82	-193.59	346.35	346.35
10. Accumulated Loss (-)/ Profit (Rs. in crore)	-1505.60	-1422.71	-1082.96	-1739.28	-2272.60	-2872.60

Source: *Reports of the Comptroller and Auditor General of India (Commercial), on Andhra Pradesh for 1998-99 to 2003-04.*

Location and creation of new enterprises: It is advisable that location and creation of-new-enterprises is examined by an expert body before a political decision is taken. In the absence of that, a few enterprises suffer from inherent disadvantages.

Internal resource mobilisation and surplus utilisation: It will be advisable for the Government to encourage Public Enterprises to maximise their own activity. This will go a long way in encouraging the managements of the Corporations to generate more internal resources. Government should tap only the return on the investment by way of dividend and through tax for their other purposes.

In recent years, the financial performance of the SLPEs has touched the rock bottom. Table 1 depicts the financial performance of the SLPEs in AP.

3

Development and Performance of State Level Public Enterprises in Assam

*R.K. Barua**

Assam is the most important state of the Indian Union in the north eastern. SLPEs were conspicuous by their absence in the state before 1954. However, the number of public enterprises shot up to 44 in 1987. The paper discusses the genesis and growth of the SLPEs in Assam and the manner in which their objectives differ from their counterpart in other states. The paper points out the poor financial performance of the SLPEs and holds the lack of application of the modern management system responsible for the existence. The paper advocates for more autonomy to the SLPEs both in terms of policy parameter and business procedures. It highlights the limitations of the Accountant General's control over the SLPEB. It also expresses the concern about inordinate delay in the preparation and finalisation of Accounts in the SLPEs.

Genesis and Growth of State Level Public Enterprises in Assam

Assam, including present-day Meghalaya, Mizoram, and Nagaland, did not have any State Level Public Enterprises (SLPE) in the pre-independence period. This was one dimension

* Secretary to Department of Public Enterprises, Government of Assam.

of the larger reality that industrialisation itself was almost non- existent in Assam in those days barring brisk activity in three sectors. First, Assam had a small but the only Petroleum Refinery in the country at Digboi. Secondly, most of the about 800 tea-gardens had their small captive tea factories. The third sector comprised of a few rice mills and mustard oil mills in the small townships of Assam. When it is remembered that the tea factories were seasonal and were in reality, only extensions of tea plantations and without links with surrounding area, it becomes obvious that pre-independence Assam including present day Meghalaya, Mizoram and Nagaland was indeed a big rural, unindustrialized region.

This state of affairs was partly due to the fact that in those days the North-Eastern region was a hinterland of industrially developed metropolitan Calcutta. Consequently. the forward and backward linkages adversely affected Assam in those days. In the secio-economic milleue of a peasant economy, there was no scope either for ushering in industrialisation by out- siders nor for growth of local entrepreneurs.

One major policy of the State Government after independence was to industrialise the State. But politicians and bureaucrats of the then Assam had no experience of establishing and managing industries. However, the erstwhile politicians being rooted to the soil, instinctively realised that in the socio-economic millien of Assam, the State Government must act as the surrogate entrepreneur and industrialist al beit their limited horizon.

Naturally, the Industrial Policy of those days was mainly restricted to encouragement of cottage and tiny industries that could use locally available raw materials like bamboo, wood, silk etc. A few small-scale industrial units set up by the Government as Departmental Undertakings in the early years were of the same variety. The only enterprise of different sort that the Government had to takeover from the British owners was the Transport Undertaking that served as the only link between Shillong, the then capital of Assam, with rest of the country. But that too was a small undertaking with a fleet of few vehicles covering only a 100 KM long route.

It was in the fitness of things that the first SLPE was the statutory Assam Financial Corporation set up in 1954. The then Government realised that in view of its meagre budgetary resources, it will have to encourage private sector industrialists and entrepreneurs by making finances easily available through such bodies. The second SLPE set up next year, though it can hardly be called an enterprise in the usual sense, was the Khadi and Village Industries Board. Thus feasibility of introducing moderably large SLPEs took time to develop a real SLPE, a Co-operative Sugar Mill, was commissioned in 1958.

Table 3.1 gives the names of SLPEs with years in which those were set up years of commissioning and the original authorised capital. Three broad facts emerge therefrom:

(a) Leaving aside the Assam State Electricity Board and Assam State Transport Corporation, the other SLPEs are rather small concerns.

(b) The rate of setting up of SLPEs till 1985 was about one SLPE in a year. This rate has been accelerated from the last year as evidenced by the fact that the Public Enter- prise Board of the State Government has cleared 14 projects since February 1986. These are in various stages of implementation. A few more projects are presently under consideration of the Public Investment Board.

(c) The general trend has been towards setting up larger

enterprises and to catering to varied interests of the State.

Objectives of the State Level Public Enterprises

One of the basic objectives of industrial policy of socialist-minded government in the third-world countries is to control the commanding hights of the economy. The State Government in Assam has, however not conceived the possibility of controlling the commanding heights of the State economy. Rather, the State Government being always poor in financial resources, though not in physical resources, it has not been possible to go for investments to make it even the leading entrepreneurs and industrialist.

In respect of other basic objectives of setting up SLPEs, Assam's case is perhaps slightly different from some other sister States. Assam's economy even now remains mainly agricultural and as such, a major aim of the SLPEs is to open avenues of employment of the growing work-force and increase the national income of the State. Another aim is to exploit the natural resources which would otherwise remain ununder-utilised. The third aim is to generate surplus to augment the State's poor financial resources foiundertaking further developmental activities. A fourth aim, is to increase the welfare of the people by offering services in which the State is lacking. A fifth aim is for the Government to intervene in those production sectors where public interest so demands. A sixth aim in setting up a few welfare-oriented enterprises has been to create business-like organisations to supplement the welfare activities of the Government efficiently and effectively.

In addition to these basic goals, each enterprise has its own individual aims and objectives. A point need to be mentioned in this context. Just as the same or similar Plan Schemes under all sectors appear in all State Five Year Plans.

Similarly the States tend to establish similar SLPEs with perhaps marginal modifications. Hence, there may not be much individuality in aims and objectives of the individual SLPEs in Assam as the following brief discussions reveal.

The Statutory SLPEs

There are six statutory SLPEs in fields of electricity, transport, warehousing, financ'e, housing and handlooms. Being born of the same or similar statutes, their aims and objectives are the same allover the country. In some of these, e.g., in the transport and warehousing sectors, joint participation by the Government of India and the State Government in' equity-holding is statutorily provided.

The Agro-Based and Aineral-Based Industries etc.

There are three sugar mills, one Khandsart mill. one jute mill and one mineral development corporation. The aims of these SLPEs is to exploit the natural resources locally available. Another SLPE. the Agro-Industries Development Corporation, as its name indicates is to assist the agricultural sector by-providing machines equipments, fertilizers, etc.

The Plantation Industries

The Assam Tea Corporation was established to undertake salvage operations, viz., to takeover sick private-sector tea-estates and to rejuvenate those. Subsequently, it brought a few estates from their British owners. The Plantation Crop Development Corporation mainly aims to develop coffee and rubber plantations in the two hill districts of Assam to wean away the tribal cultivators from the ruinous humming practices. The Assam seeds corporation is to assist agricultural development by growing and distributing improved seeds.

The Manufacturing Sector

These SLPEs constitute the largest sector with thirteen units. This sector includes textile mills, fertiliser factories, engineering units, electronic industry, gas and petro-chemical based industries. Only a few of these use raw materials brought from outside the state. Others have been set up mainly to utilise local raw materials.

Promotional SLPEs

There are three non-financial enterprises set up with the aim of promoting industrialisation in both public and private sectors in three specified areas, viz., (a) medium and large scale units, (b) small scale units and (c) small scale units in the hill districts. Each of them has a few units as either subsidiaries or their production wings. Two financial institutions serve the same purpose through their lending activities.

Fishery and Livestock Units

The Fisheries Development Corporation aims to develop inland fisheries on scientific lines with adequate investments to increase supply of fish and to improve the conditions of fisher- man community. The Livestock Corporation aims to undertake both production and marketing of livestock & poultry products.

Welfare-Oriented Industries

There are three SLPEs for accelerating development of Scheduled Castes, Plains Tribals and Other Backward Classes by encouraging them to take up mainly tiny and small-scale industrial and commercial ventures. These SLPEs can avail of the large-scale resources of financial institutions to augment their resources. These SLPEs can, therefore, step in where the State's Departmental activities in these spheres require support.

Miscellaneous SLPEs

There are two commercial organisations. The STATFED mainly operates in fields of essential commodities to ensure reasonable prices and to keep the private sector under control.

The second commercial corporation aims to market the products of tinyand small-scale units and thus improve the financial conditions of the skilled artisans etc. The Assam Government Construction Corporation is to act as deterrant to growth of monopoly interests in construction trades and to curb profit-mongering by private contractors. The very names of the Assam Textbook Production and Publication Corporation, The Minor Irrigation Development Corporation and the Police Housing Corporation indicate the major aims of those Corporations.

Summing Up

The variety of SLPEs under the State Government may appear surprising. This is, however, natural in the sense that each of those have been set up to meet some urgent public interest from time to time. This is also partly due to the fact that the entrepreneur class is not yet developed in Assam.

Organisational Structures and Sectorwise Classification

As has been mentioned earlier, the SLPEs have been established over a long period since 1954 in diverse fields of activity. Their organisational structures are also different. Table 3.2 gives the organisational category-wise break-up of the SLPEs. The table shows that the government has preference for government companies. In fact, the new industrial projects that are going to be set up in near future will be government companies. It need to be emphasized that though the enterprises under the co-operative sector were established due to enthusiasm of individual cooperators, those have turned out to be cooperatives only in name. The role of individual cooperator in equity participation has become hardly noticeable. Management of these companies has also been taken over by the government under provisions of the Cooperative Act. This strange situation obtaining in Assam reflects the absence of a genuine and successful co-operative movement in Assam. This is why these societies are treated as SLPEs in Assam while that may not be the case in the states where vigorous cooperative governments exist. Sector-wise classification of SLPEs are given in Table 3.3.

An important point to be remembered in regard to the sector-wise classification of SLPEs is the fact that these categories must not be taken as water-tight compartments. A few SLPEs have more than one function which entitle them to be classified in different sectors. Five examples will clarify the position. The Assam Agro-Industries Corporation not only produces agricultural tools and equipments but also trade in fertilizers and tractors. The ASIDC Ltd. and the AHSIDC Ltd. promote industries but each has a few small-scale departmentally-run manufacturing units. The AGMC has both production and marketing activities. The STATFED is mainly a trading enterprise but has a few captive manufacturing units. However. the SLPEs have been classified in Table 6.3 according to the main line of activity of each SLPE.

Investments and Sources

There are five sources of investment capital in SLPEs in Assam as given below :

1. State Government: (a) Equity Capital
   (b) Short-term loan (other than working capital
   (c) Long-term loan
   (d) Grants and subsidies,
2. Financial Institutions:Term loan
3. Union Government: (a) Term Capital
   (b) Industrial subsidy
4. Public/market: (a) Equity capital
   (b) Loan through banks

5. SLPEs: Internal resources for expansion and diversification

4.2 Of the above sources, the role of l(b), l(d), 3(b), 4 and 5 need to be briefly mentioned.

(i) Short term loans: These loans are given to enable the SLPEs to tide over temporary ways and means difficulties. The assumption is that the loans will be cleared as soon as the financial situation improved. The amounts so lent is not large. Nor is it the usual practice to go for this sort of financing. However, the point to be noted is that in cases of chronically sick units, this type of loan remains pending for years and finally gets converted to either equity or long-term loan.

(ii) Grants and subsidies : The state government as a rule does not offer grants or subsidies to the SLPEs. But the units in the cooperative sector may claim benefits admissible to them as cooperative societies and they may obtain managerial and other subsidies. The amounts involved, however, are not large.

(iii) Industrial subsidy: This is what is admissible as incentive to new industrial units set up in industrially backward regions. The maximum limit for an unit is Rs. 25 lakhs only.

(iv) Equity contribution by Public and Borrowing through Bonds :

The Government companies in Assam are not open for equity participation by the Public. Besides, the concept of the joint sector is yet to be implemented in Assam. Hence, the negligible amount of equity participation in the SLPEs comes mainly from the contribution by the individual cooperators in the SLPEs in the cooperative sector. Only the Assam State Electricity Board raises loan from market by issuing bonds.

The question of investment of surplus generated by the

SLPEs may arise when healthy units go for expansion or diversification. Both these conditions are not satisfied in case of the SLPEs in Assam. Only now three SLPEs are in a position to partly finance their expansion activities.

Financial Performance of SLPEs

Table 3 4 gives the profit and loss position of the SLPEs for five years from 1980-81 to 1984-85. The total net loss of all SLPEs together during this period comes to Rs. 8467 lakhs. This is quite substantial for a financially poor state like Assam. Table 3.5 also gives sector-wise profit and loss position. It is seen that SLPEs in only two sectors, commercial and construction, earn profits sector-wise. Out of the 44 SLPEs, a few are new enterprises which were not commissioned by 1985-86. Hence the losses shown against them during this period are losses of the preoperative period. Therefore, losses of these units should be left out of consideration when financial returns of SLPEs are examined. The following SLPEs belong to this category ;

(a) Assam Syntex Ltd.
(b) Assam Electronic Development Corporation
(c) Assam Polytext Ltd.
(d) S.K.K. Sutakel Ltd.
(e) Assam Co-operative Spinning Mills Ltd.
(f) Assam Polyester Co-operative Spinning Mill.
(g) Nowgong Sugar Mill
(h) Assam State Textile Corporation
(i) Assam Mineral Development Corporation
(j) Assam Livestock & Poulty Development Corporation
(k) Assam Fisheries Development Corporation

It will however be noted that the combined loss incurred

by this group not being large, their exclusion will not substantially alter the overall financial position of the SLPEs. The seriousness of the situation is brought to a focus in the following table compiled from Table 3.6.

TABLE 3.6

(a)	No.of SLPEs not commissioned	11
(b)	No.of SLPEs with inadequate data	3
(c)	No.of SLPEs not incurring loss	3
(d)	No.of SLPEs incurring loss in 1 year	6
(e)	No.of SLPEs incurring loss in 2 years	3
(f)	No.of SLPEs incurring loss in 3 years	1
(g)	No.of SLPEs incurring loss in 4 years	6
(h)	No.of SLPEs incurring loss in 5 years	11

In group (b) are three SLPEs which have not furnished data for 2 or more years within the 5 year period beginning with 1980-81. This group and the new SLPEs which are in the gestation stage or have been commissioned in the last one or two years of the period are left out of the groupings from (c) to (h) of the table.

Out of the remaining 31 SLPEs, 11 have incurred losses during the whole period, 6 in 4 years, 1 in 3 years, 3 in 2 years and 6 in one year while only three have not incurred any loss during this period. It may be noted that in category 'g' i.e., incurring loss for four years, there are 3 SLPEs out of 5 in this group which have one year with 'NA' (not available) mark which means that it is quite likely that these three units really belong to the next group incurring losses during the whole period. The best example of this sub-group is the Assam State Transport Corporation which has incurred a loss of Rs. 1354 lakhs in 4 years for which figures are available. In other words, the situation is even more serious than the one revealed by Table 3.5.

It has been mentioned earlier that most of the SLPEs in Assam are of small size. This is reflected by the magnitude of loss 'incurred'. Generally, bigger the unit, larger is the loss.

TABLE 3.7

List of Large-Scale Public Enterprises

SLPEs	*Years Covered*	*Loss (in Rs. lakhs)*
Assam State Electricity Board	5	4781
Assam Road Transport Corporation	4	1354
Assam Tea Corporation	5	980
Cachar Sugar Mill	Total	7771

These 4 units contribute 91.78% of total loss incurred during the period. Of these, Assam Tea Corporation is saddled with some sick gardens taken over from the private sectors. Cachar Sugar Mill is not a large unit but it has practically been a non-starter from the very beginning. In the next group are 6 SLPEs which incur loss in between Rs. 150 lakhs and Rs. 225 lakhs during the period. The remaining loss-incurring SLPEs are small units incurring small losses.

There are three units that have not incurred any loss during this period. The Film (Finance & Development) Corporation operate with capital fund of Rs. 10 lakh only and has so far lent money to few producers/ directors of films. The second SLPEs is the Assam State Warehousing Corporation and the nature of its activities makes it a profit-earning unit. The third profit-yielding SLPEs is the Assam Government Construction Corporation which is practically a Civil Contractor Firm. As such, it could have earned larger profit than Rs. 30 lakhs in 5 years. Besides, its performance has not been uniform over the years. A fourth unit, the Assam Gas Company has been put in category 'd' but it should really be in category 'c' because the loss incurred in one year is only Rs. 19,000. In fact, it has generally been a profit-earning unit.

In a similar situation is the Assam Financial Corporation which has been placed in group 'd'. Another unit of group 'd' viz., Assam Petro-chemical Ltd. was losing in earlier years but it turned corner during this period. The Text Book Production and Publication Board could be in category 'c' instead of being in 'd' if it is properly managed.

Sickness of enterprises and specially of Public Enterprises has become a common phenomenon in India. Many studies made by different specialists and institutions into the causes of their sickness come to one conclusion, viz.. The major culprit for sickness of Indian enterprises is managerial failure. The same appears to be the case of the SLPEs in Assam. Perhaps the situation in Assam is compounded by non-professionalised approach of the Government to t~ problems of SLPEs and the general disabilities that grow out of economic backwardness of the state like lack of industrial culture. However, there is no need for cynicism. A recent experiment clearly illustrates the position. The Assam Cooperative Jute Mill was commissioned in 1971 and it had all the reasons to be successful. Raw-jute was available at the factory-gate and so also was the market for its products. The machineries were new imported and of the best quality. The workers were new to the job but could be trained and shaped as the management desired. But the Mill's performance was bad from the early years. The rate of capacity utilisation was very low and it was the result of weaknesses in almost all spheres. All this made the Mill chronically sick and finally it was closed down in 1984. Then in the context of the Assam Accord it was opened in late 1985 with a competent expert as the Chairman-cum-Managing Director. The Mill appears to be about to turn corner within this short span of time with the same workers and the same machinery etc. The only change has been at the Management level.

Status of SLPES in Assam

Table 3.8 explains about the financial performance of SLPEs in Assam:

TABLE 3.8

Status of SLPEs in Assam

Items	*Years*	*2000-01*	*2001-002*	*2002-03*	*2003-04*	*2004-05*
1.	Total no. of SLPEs*	42	42	42	42	43
2.	No.of Working SLPEs	32	32	32	32	33
3.	No.of Non-Working SLPEs	10	10	10	10	10
	(i) Under Liquidation					
	(ii) Under Closure					
	(iii) Under Merger					
	(iv) Others					
4.	Total Equity	1774.41	1785.32	1786.14	1786.65	1786.91
5.	Total Debt	2155.13	2267.60	2306.88	583.30	2556.07
6.	Total Investment	3929.54	4052.98	4093.00	2369.95	4342.98
7.	No.of Profit making enterprises	6	7	8	9	11
8.	No.of Loss making enterprises	36	35	34	33	32
9.	Net Profit/Loss	-785.26	-735.43	-691.61	-727.47	-670.93
10.	Accumulated Loss(-)/Profit		-3589.71	-4944.40	-4593.01	-5268.40

Source: *Reports of the Comptroller and Auditor General of India (Commercial), on Assam. For 2000-01 to 2004-05.*

Control System and Internal Management Systems

Control System

The control system of the SLPEs in Assam is the same as elsewhere in the country but some variations may occur in exercising the controls. The present position in this regard is briefly discussed below.

Though the Annual Reports on the Government Companies are to be regularly placed before the State Assembly, this has not yet been done in Assam. This has, however, not prevented the State Legislature from taking active interest in the affairs of the SLPEs, monitoring and evaluating their activities and offering guidelines to the government in the matter.

The Committee on Public Undertakings (COPU) of the State Assembly has been conducting in-depth studies of individual SLPEs. The general approach and business procedures of the committee are not different from those of their counterparts in other State Legislatures. The Committee has so far released reports which contain its findings as well as recommendations about the SLPEs. The Committee also monitors and evaluates the progress in implementing its recommendations by the Government.

There are 14 Secretariat Departments which have SLPEs under their administrative control. The Industries Department has the largest number of SLPEs under it while a few departments (e.g., Education, PWD) have only one or two SLPEs under them. The Administrative Departments appoint the Board of Directors, the Chairman and the Managing Director. The SLPEs have freedom to appoint personnel except the senior ones. It has been found that the SLPEs under efficient Board of Directors and Managing Directors generally take important decisions within their powers without seeking prior approval of the Government. This is facilitated by the fact that generally senior officers of the Administrative Departments and the Finance Department are members of the Board of Directors. However, where decisions involve commitment of large funds, approval of the Government has to be sought. In many areas, the powers of the Board has been limited (e.g., in revision of pay-scales) as otherwise general imbalance in pay-structures in government services and the SLPEs may occur. The sick SLPEs have, of course, to come to the Government frequently as they have to depend on funds released by the Government. However, there is no denying that the autonomy by the SLPEs is also limited by certain policy parameters and business procedures of the Government. For example, it is difficult to retrench surplus work-force; the Rules about reservation of jobs for weaker sections have to be followed; the amounts expected from the Government in a year will have to be included in the Budget for that year and lot of formalities will have to be observed at that stage and subsequently when funds are to be released. Further, on issues like undue interferences by the Government or back-seat driving by the bureaucrats in the Administrative Departments, the situation appears not to be basically different from what obtains in the rest of the country.

The role of the Finance Department is limited to financial affairs of the SLPEs but since all schemes involve finance, the Finance Department may be said to have vast control over functioning of the SLPEs. It is also a fact that the Finance Department may not always have the required managerial expertise to view the problems from wider angles. However, there appears to be only a few, if any, instances in Assam where the Finance Department can be said to have been the stumbling block in growth and development of SLPEs.

The Department of Public Enterprises is the nodal agency in the State Government in regard to the SLPEs. It is modeled after the Bureau of Public Enterprises, Government of India. However, though created in 1976, it is being properly strengthened only now by recruiting a good number of experts in various management fields. The Department is to act as the eyes and ears of the Government in respect of the SLPEs and advise and guide the Government and the SLPEs about actions to be taken for improving and developing the SLPEs. In fact) the existing rules give ample powers to the Department of Public Enterprises to positively intervene in all major policy matters relating to the SLPEs. Since there is no other agency within the Government with such expertise and placed in such advantageous position) the Department will have to play a major role as the controlling and guiding agency in years to come.

The Department of Public Enterprises also acts as the Secretariat to the Public Investment Board and the Public Enterprises. Selection Board which have been created after the two bodies with identical names in the Government of India.

The control exercised by the Accountant General in respect of the SLPEs in Assam has not been appreciable 80 far. The comments on the audited Balance-sheets come too late to be of much use to the Management as part of the managerial MIS. However, as in the case of the Public Accounts Committee those comments can be used by the Government for taking remedial actions in many important fields.

Internal Management Systems

The reflection of the general backwardness of Assam may be traced to the management systems of the SLPEs. The business-like work-culture is yet to penetrate into most of the SLPEs. This situation is epitomised in the fact that professionalisation of management is still a distant goal in Assam. A few examples will suffice to clarify the position. Most of the Managing Directors are deputationists from the organised Administrative Services who may not have any previous experience in management of enterprises and they are frequently transferred. Distinction between financial management and book-keeping is yet to be recognised in most of the SLPEs. MIS is still an unknown quantity in SLPEs in Assam. None of the SLPEs has a Cost Accountant in its roll and only a couple of SLPEs have availed of the services of Cost Accountants for adhoc purposes. The job of Personnel Manager in most SLPEs is performed by the concerned Administrative Officers who generally happens to be a generalist of junior rank. But it need be emphasised that while absence of professionalisation and business-like work-culture have hindered adoption of modern and effective management practices and control systems, it is equally true that professionally qualified personnel are not easily available in Assam due to its general backwardness.

Perhaps a mention of Internal Audit system may be made as an illustration. It is a known technique and many SLPEs utilise it. But the system is designed to serve only accounting purposes but not financial management purposes.

However most of the SLPEs in Assam being rather small units, it is possible to exaggerate the role of many such modern management skills and techniques. For example the only Jute Mill in Assam being a small unit. An effective Managing Director is in a position to exercise managerial control without introducing highly sophisticated techniques or recruiting a bunch of specialists.

Boards of Management

The power of appointing the Boards of Management in Statutory Corporations and Government Companies vests in the Government. This power as regards the SLPEs in the Cooperative sector has also been taken over by the Government. The number of members of the Boards in case of each SLPE is determined as per provisions of the Articles of Association or relevant rules of the SLPEs. The Board of the Assam State Electricity Board consists of 3 to 7 members. In other cases, broadly speaking, around 11 members constitute the Boards.

There has been no fixed tenures for the Boards. In some cases the Boards continue for a reasonable period but in other cases, the Boards have been reconstituted frequently.

The composition of the Boards is generally of the following pattern:

(a) One representative of the Administrative Department

(b) One from the Finance Department

(c) A few members from other related Government Departments and Directorates

(d) A few MLAs/Politicians having knowledge and interests in the fields of the concerned SLPEs

(e) Some experts in the fields of the concerned SLPEs

(f) One or two representatives from concerned agencies of Government of India

(g) The Managing Director of the SLPE.

Within this pattern, variations occur. For example; in some Boards the politicians may preponderate while in some others, the officials may constitute the majority.

The concerned Administrative Departments are to consult the Department of Public Enterprises in appointing the Board of Directors, the Chairman and the Managing Director.

One of the members of the Board is appointed simultaneously as the Chairman by the Government. In a few cases the Ministers and senior Government Officers of the concerned Departments are appointed as the Chairmen.

Norms of the Government of India have been broadly followed in determining the emoluments of the Chairmen. The Ministers and the Government Officials do not get any emolument as Chairmen. The part-time non-official Chairman receives Rs. 1000.00 pm as honorarium, a car with a driver, 75 litres of petrol per month for movements in the H.Q. of the SLPEs, TA/DA at rates admissible to Class I Government servants, a phone at residence and a peon to work at his bunglow.

The non-official members of the Boards get sitting fees

and TA/DA. The rates vary among the SLPEs. The Government is now considering standardisation of these rates. The Official members of the Boards are not entitled to receive sitting fees.

There is no fixed norm about frequency of holding meetings of the Board. But as issues requiring decision of the Boards are many, the meetings are generally held quarterly.

There is no generalised procedure of organising interface between the Boards and concerned agencies of the Government but the Chairmen keep close contact with the Government agencies. The role of the part-time non-official Chairman is, however, still to be clearly defined.

Special Issues: Resource Development

Assam being an economically backward region opportunities for skill-formation are also lagging in Assam. It may be broadly said that presently there is no gap between demand for and supply of general skills. The situation becomes difficult when specific skills are demand, e.g., demand for skilled carpenters welders fitters etc., and at higher levels Cost Accountants, Productional Engineers etc.

The SLPEs and the Government are aware of these defficiencies and are taking various steps to remedy the situation by designing appropriate training programmes for upgrading skills of the existing employees at all levels. In several new SLPEs e.g., the Polyester Spinning Mills the training programme has been built into the pre-operative phase of the project itself whereby trainee-officers arid workers are recruited and sent for training in Mills elsewhere in the country during the gestation period of the project. There is, however, no doubt that there remainsa lot of things to be done though in-service trainings to improve productivity of the employees for the benefit of both employees and the organisations.

As has been discussed earlier, modern management

techniques are still to be employed in SLPEs in Assam and the same holds true of the procedure applied for selection, appointment and promotion of employees. Similarly, rough and ready measures are still applied for performance evaluation.

The general norm is determining emoluments in the SLPEs is that large-scale imbalance between pay-scales in the Government services and the SLPEs should not occur. Most of the SLPEs follow the Government pay-scales and allowances with some variations. In cases of pay revisions consequential to revision of pay-scales of Government servants, the SLPEs follow Government instructions about revision of their pay-scales. As regards wages of the working class, only a handful of the SLPEs have adopted wage fixation through collective bargaining. The Government is aware that the system now in vogue is not very appropriate and is presently considering the proposal to set up a pay-committee to go into the details of the emoluments of the SLPEs.

Investment Decisions

Proposals for setting up of new SLPEs or large-scale expansion of existing SLPEs are placed before the Public Investment Board by the Administrative Departments that act as the promoters. The Department of Public Enterprises act as the Secretariat to this committee. The recommendations of the committee are placed before the Departmental Ministers and the cabinet for final decision.

The SLPEs may, however, take investment decisions on developmental schemes with smaller financial involvement. The relevant Rule in this respect is that where the investment proposal is of less than Rs. 25 lakhs, the matter need not be placed before the PIB. The SLPEs, however, generally obtain approval of the concerned Administrative Departments before implementing new schemes/projects though it may not be strictly required when representatives of the Administrative Departments and Finance Department sit on the Boards of Directors.

Product-mix Decisions

In case of new SLPEs, the proposed product-mix is considered and approved by the Public Investment Board while approving the project itself. In other cases, the decisions about product-mix are taken by the Board of Directors of the SLPEs.

Location

The promoter of the new SLPEs, generally an Administrative Department or an existing SLPE, rises the issue of location in the Project Report and discusses the merits and demerits of the selected location. In making such selections, the promoters take into account not only financial aspects but also other significant socio-economic aspects like bringing industries to specially depressed or backward regions. In fact, the state government has consciously taken the policy decision of wide dispersal of SLPEs without, of course, jeopardizing financial viability of the projects.

TABLE 3.1

Year of Formation and with Authorised Capital of SLPEs

Year of Formation		*Name of SLPEs*	*Authorised Capital*
1		2	3
1954	1.	Assam Financial Corporation	200
1955	2.	Assam Khadi and Village Industries Board	Loans and Grants taken from time to time
	3.	Assam Cooperative Sugar Mills Ltd.	200
1958	4.	Assam State Warehousing Corporation	200
1959	5.	Chemical Unit of Associated Industries Ltd.	Sick Private sector unit taken over

Year	No.	Name	Amount
	6.	Assam Government Marketing Corporation Ltd.	100
1960	7.	Assam Co-operative Jute Mills Ltd.	500
	8.	Assam Spun Silk Mills Ltd.	85
1962	9.	Assam Small Industries Dev. Corpn.	200
	10.	Assam Gas Company	300
1964	11.	Assam Conductors & Tubes Ltd.	25
	12.	Assam Government Construction Corporation Ltd.	200
1965	13.	Assam Industrial Development Corporation Ltd.	500
1967	14.	Assam Agro Industries Dev. Corporation	250
	15.	Assam Seed Corporation Ltd.	100
1968	16.	Assam Hills Small Industries Dev. Corporation Ltd.	50
	17.	Uttar Assam Samabai Chenikol Ltd.	300
1970	18.	Assam State Transport Corpn. Ltd.	Only term loan
1971	19.	Assam Petro Chemicals Ltd.	500
	20.	Cachar Sugar Mills Ltd.	200
1972	21.	Assam State Text Book Production and Publication Corporation	50
	22.	Assam Tea Corporation	200
1974	23.	Assam State Film (Finance & Dev.) Corporation Ltd.	10
	24.	Fertichem Ltd.	50
	25.	Assam Plantation Corporation Dev. Corporation Ltd.	500
	26.	Assam State Housing Board	Loans and Grants
1975	27.	Assam Plain Tribes Development Corporation Ltd.	100
	28.	Assam State Development Corporation for S.C. Ltd.	100
	29.	Assam State Development Corporation for O.B.C Ltd.	100
	30.	Assam State Marketing & Consumers Federation Ltd. (STATFED)	300
	31.	Nowgoing Co-operative Sugar Mills Ltd.	600
	32.	Assam State Electricity Board (Successful body after Reorganisation of Assam)	Loans only
1977	33.	Assam Fisheries Development Corporation Ltd.	50
1979	34.	Saheed Kushal Konwar Samabai Sutakol Ltd.	500
	35.	Assam Co-operative Spinning Mills Ltd.	500
1980	36.	Assam State Textile Corporation Ltd.	900
	37.	Assam State Minor Irrigation Dev. Corporation Ltd.	
1981	38.	Assam Police Housing Corporation Ltd.	20
	39.	Assam Polyter Co-operative Society Spinning Mills Ltd.	500

1982	40.	Assam Syntex Ltd.	400
	41.	Assam Polytex Ltd.	600
1983	42.	Assam Mineral Development Corpn. Ltd.	20
1984	43.	Assam Electronic Dev. Corporation Ltd.	500
	44	Assam Livestock & Poultry Development Corporation Ltd.	200

TABLE 3.2

Organisational Category-wise Break-up of State Level Public Enterprises

Categories		*SLPEs*
1. Statutory Corporations	1.	Assam State Electricity Board
	2.	Assam State Transport Corporation
	3.	Assam State Warehousing Corporation
	4.	Assam Khadi & Village Industries Board
	5.	Assam Housing Board
	6.	Assam Financial Corporation
II. Government Companies	1.	Chemical Unit of Associated Industries
	2.	Assam Spun Silk Mills
	3.	Assam Small Industries Dev. Corporation
	4.	Assam Gas Company
	5.	Assam Conductors & Tubes Ltd.
	6.	Assam Government Construction Corpn.
	7.	Assam Industrial Development Corpn.
	8.	Assam Agro-Industries Dev. Corporation
	9.	Assam Seeds Corporation
	10.	Assam Hills Small Industries Development Corporation
	11.	Assam Petro-chemical Ltd.
	12.	Cachar Sugar Mills
	13.	Assam Textbook Production & Publication Corporation Ltd.
	14.	Assam Tea Corporation
	15.	Assam State Film (Finance & Development) Corporation
	16.	Fertichem Limited
	17.	Assam Plantation Crop Development Corporation
	18.	Assam Plains Tribes Development Corpn.
	19.	Assam State Development Corporation for O.B.C Ltd.

	20. Assam State Development Corporation for Scheduled Castes
	21. Assam Fisheries Development Corporation
	22. Assam State Textile Corporation
	23. Assam State Minor Irrigation Development Corporation
	24. Assam Police Housing Corporation
	25. Assam Syntex Limited
	26. Assam Polytex Limited
	27. Assam Mineral Development Corporation
	28. Assam Electronic Development Corpn.
	29. Assam Livestock & Poultry Development Corporation
	30. Assam Government Marketing Corporation
III. Co-operative Sector	1. Assam Co-operative Sugar Mills
	2. Assam Co-operative Jute Mills
	3. Uttar Assam Samabai Chenikol
	4. STATFED
	5. Nowgong Co-operative Sugar Mill
	6. S.K.K. Samabai Sutakol
	7. Assam Cooperative Spinning Mills
	8. Assam Polyster Cooperative Ltd.

TABLE 3.3

Sector-wise Classification of SLPEs

Categories	*SLPEs*
I. Promotional (including these offering financial assistance)	1. Assam Industrial Development Corpn.
	2. Assam Small Industries Dev. Corpn.
	3. Assam Hills Small Industries Dev. Corporation
	4. Assam Financial Corporation
	5. Assam Film (Finance & Dev.) Corpn.
II. Manufacturing	1. Assam Cooperative Sugar Mills
	2. Chemical Unit of Associated Industries
	3. Assam Cooperative Jute Mills
	4. Assam Spun Silk Mills
	5. Assam Gas Company
	6. Assam Conductors and Tubes Ltd.
	7. Assam Agro Industries Development Corporation
	8. Uttar Asom Samabai Chenikol

	9. Assam Petro-Chemical Ltd.
	10. Cachar Sugar Mills
	11. Fertichem Limited
	12. Nowgong Cooperative Sugar Mills
	13. S.K.K. Samabai Sutakol
	14. Assam Cooperative Spinning Mills
	15. Assam State Textile Corporation
	16. Assam Polyester Cooperative Spinning Mills
	17. Assam Syntex Ltd.
	18. Assam Polytex Ltd.
	19. Assam Electronic Development Corpn.
III. Commercial	1. STATFED
	2. Assam Government Marketing Corpn.
	3. Assam Warehousing Development Corpn.
IV. Plantation	1. Assam Tea Corporation
	2. Assam Plantation Crop Development Corporation
	3. Assam Seeds Corporation
V. Mining	1. Assam Mineral Development Corpn.
VI. Construction	1. Assam Government Construction Corpn.
	2. Assam Police Housing Corporation
VII. Services	1. Assam State Electricity Board
	2. Assam State Transport Corporation
VIII. Welfare-oriented	1. Assam Plains Tribals Dev. Corpn.
	2. Assam State Development Corporation for O.B.C. Limited
	3. Assam State Development Corporation for Scheduled Castes.
IX. Miscellaneous	1. Assam Textbook Production and Publication Corporation
	2. Assam Khadi & Village Industries Board
	3. Assam State Housing Board
	4. Assam Fisheries Development Corpn.
	5. Assam Livestock & Poultry Development Corporation
	6. Assam State Minor Irrigation Development Corporation

TABLE 3.4

Financial Structure of SLPEs

(Rs. in Lakhs)

SLPEs	As on	Equity	Subsidy & Grant	Loan Short term	Loan Long term	Total
1	2	3	4	5	6	7
1. Assam Industrial Development Corporation	31-3-86	500	--	--	3158	3658
2. Assam Small Industries Development Corporation	31-3-85	193		73	44	310
3. Assam Hills Indusries Development Corporation	31-3-85	200	--	--	221	421
4. Assam Financial Corporation	31-3-87	367	--	--	1527	1894
5. Assam Film (Finance & Development Corporation	31-3-85	5	--	--	5	10
6. Assam Co-op Sugar Mill	30-6-86	193	--	--	419	612
7. Chemical Unit of AIA	31-3-86	60	--	--	415	475
8. Assam Co-op. Jute Mill	30-3-85	180	--	15	113	308
9. Assam Spun Silk Mill	31-3-86	8	--	--	53	133
10. Assam Gas Company	31-3-86	248	--	599	2068	2915
11. Assam Conductors & Tubes	31-3-86	6	--	--	102	108
12. Uttar A.S. Chenikel	30-6-82	6	--	--	8	14
13. Assam Petro-Chemicals	31-3-86	500	2	--	472	974
14. Assam Agro-Indusries Development Corporation	31-3-84	220	--	330	--	550
15. Cachar Sugar Mill	31-3-86	338	119	--	1124	1581
16. Fertichem Ltd.	31-3-86	18	--	--	310	328
17. Nagaon Co-op Sugar Mills	A s	623	25	--	542	1190

18.	S.K.K. Soautakol	i	444	--	--	444	888
		n					
19.	Assam Co-op. Spinning Mill	p	465	--	--	465	930
		r					
20.	Assam State Textile Corporation	o	645	25	--	465	1135
		j					
21.	Assam Polyester Co-operative Spinning Mill	e c	400	20	--	630	1050
		t					
22.	Assam Syntex Limited	r	512	25	--	460	997
		e					
23.	Assam Polytex Ltd.	p	517	25	--	450	992
		o					
24.	Assam Electronic Development Corporation Stateed	r	5	--	--	--	5
		t					
25.	Stateed	31-3-86	518	121	546	8240	9425
26.	Assam Government Marketing	31-3-86	145	--	--	149	294
27.	Assam Warehousing Corporation	31-3-86	367	--.56	--	423	
28.	Assam Tea Corporation	31-3-85	500	--	960	17	1477
29.	Assam Plantation Corporation Development Corporation	31-3-85	50	70	157	135	862
30.	Assam Seeds Corporation	31-3-86	146	--	514	441	1101
31.	Assam Mineral Development Corporation	31-3-85	20	--	--	--	20
32.	Assam Government Construction Corporation	31-3-84	50	--	--	135	185

1	2	3	4	5	6	7
33. Assam Police Housing Corporation	31-3-84	350	--	--	--	350
34. Assam State Electricity Board	31-3-85	--	--	--	73282	73282
35. Assam State Transport Corporation	31-3-84	--	23	--	1984	2007
36. Assam Plains Tribes Develoopment Corporation	31-3-84	292	--	--	--	292
37. Assam State Development Corporation for O.B.C	31-3-86	58	41	--	--	99
38. Assam State Development Corporation for S.C.	31-3-85	150	97	--	--	247
39. Assam Textile Production & Publication Corporation	31-3-85	50	--	--	59	109
40. Assam Khadi & Village Board	31-3-85	--	--	67	143	210
41. Assam Housing Board	31-3-83	88	--	--	773	861
42. Assam Fisheries Development Corporation	Project Report	150	27	--	306	483
43. Assam Livestock & Poultry Development Corporation	As in project	250	--	--	272	522
44. Assam Minor Irrigation Development Corporation	31-3-87	515	--	--	1701	2216
Total		10,874	620	3,317	1,01,132	1,15,943

TABLE-3. 5

Statement showing Profit (+) and Loss (-) of SLPEs during 1980-81 to 1984-85

Sector	SLPEs	1980-81	1981-82	1982-83	1983-84	1984-85	Total
I. Promotional	1. Assam Industrial Development Corpn.	20	-17	-19	-52	-89	-157
	2. Assam Small Industries Dev. Corpn.	-2	-3	-14	-22	-41	-82
	3. Assam Hills Small Industries Dev. Corpoation	-20	-22	-13	-5	-16	-76
	4. Assam Financial Corporation	-22	10	20	13	27	48
	5. Assam Film (Finance & Dev.) Corpn.	0.24	0.14	0.47	0.40	-0.34	-
	Sub-Total	-24	-32	-26	-66	-119	-267
II. Manufacturing	1. Assam Cooperative Sugar Mills	-9	-24	-68	-50	-55	-206
	2. Chemical Unit of A.I.A. Ltd.	-25	-28	-24	-27	-49	-153
	3. Assam Cooperative Jute Mills	-26	-38	-56	-63	-21	-204
	4. Assam Spun Silk Mills	3	7	-9	0.28	0.09	1
	5. Assam Gas Company	1	29	79	-0.19	56	174
	6. Assam Conductors and Tubes Ltd.	1	-11	3	-32	43	4
	7. Assam Agro Industries Development Corporation	-10	-1	1	1	NA	-9
	8. Uttar Asom Samabai Cahenikol Ltd.	-3.38	-1	-1	-1	NA	-3
	9. Assam Petro-Chemical Ltd.	-39	11	22	113	114	221
	10. Cachar Sugar Mills Ltd.						
	11. Fertichem Limited						
	12. Nowgong Cooperative Sugar Mills						
	13. S.K.K. Samabai Sutakol						
	14. Assam Cooperative Spinning Mills						

	15.	Asam State Textile Corporation
	16.	Assam Polyester Cooperative Spinning Mill
	17.	Assam Syntex Ltd.
	18.	Assam Polytex Ltd.
	19.	Assam Elecronic Development Corpn.
III. Commercial	1.	STATFED
	2.	Assam Goernment Marketing Corpn.
	3.	Assam Warehousing Dev. Corpn.
IV. Plantation	1.	Assam Tea Corporation
	2.	Assam Plantation Crop Development Corporation
	3.	Assam Seeds Corporation
V. Mining	1.	Assam Mineral Development Corpn.
VI. Construction	1.	Assam Government Construction Corpn.
	2.	Assam Police Housing Corporation
VII. Services	1.	Assam State Electricity Board
	2.	Assam State Transport Corporation
VIII. Welfare-oriented	1.	Assam Plains Tribels Dev. Corpn.
	2.	Assam State Development Corportion for O.B.C Limited
	3.	Assam State Development Corporation for Schedule Castes.
IX. Miscellaneous	1.	Assam Textbook Production and Publication Corportion
	2.	Assam Khadi & Village Industries Board
	3.	Assam State Housing Board
	4.	Assam Fisheries Development Corpn.
	5.	Assam Livestock & Poultry Development Corporation
	6.	Assam State Minor Irrigation Development Corporation

4

Public Sector Enterprises in Bihar: A Bird's Eye View

*Arun Prasad**

[In this paper an attempt has been made to highlight the different aspects of management and operations of the SLPEs in Bihar. The paper provides backdrop to the present happenings in the SLPEs and outlines measures to improve their performance.]

The growth of public sector in Bihar has been considered. Total investment till 85-86 is Rs. 2289.00 crores. Today there are 49 undertakings in Bihar. The number of Public Enterprises established during 1950 to 1959 was only 5. The growth in the number of Public Enterprises is given in Annexure-I which reveals that 33 Public Enterprises were set up during the period 1970-79. Table 4.1 provides data on the growth in the number of the SLPEs in Bihar.

An examination of the origin of various Public Enterprises in Bihar indicates the following broad reasons which prompted the creation of Public Enterprises.

---

* Chairman, Bureau of Public Enterprises, Government of Bihar.

** This paper has drawn heavily from the paper titled 'Management of State Level Public Enterprises in Bihar' by R K Mishra and R Nandagopal, Faculty Members, Institute of Public Enterprises, O U Campus, Hyderabad, presented at the same Seminar.

--Firstly, there are some Public Enterprises which are historical in nature e.g. the State Electricity Board and the Road Transport Corporation. Even in those days State Government felt that it was its responsibility to provide services such as electricity and urban transport.

--Secondly, some Public Enterprises were set up following a central legislation which envisaged the creation of similar institution at the State level. Bihar State Financial Corporation, Bihar State Warehousing Corporation etc. are typical examples.

--Thirdly, Public Enterprises like Agro Industries Development Corporation, Credit and Investment Corporation were set up to avail facilities which Government of India or Central Financial Institutions offered.

--Fourthly, due to nationalisation of private industry, Bihar State Sugar Corporation was set up.

--Fifthly, a number of enterprises were set up by the State Government towards sectoral development like Leather Industries Development Corporation.

--Sixthly, a number of enterprises were created for the development of the weaker sections of society like Bihar State Minorities Finance Corporation, Scheduled Caste Corporation etc.

In addition to these, other Public Enterprises established by the State Government were the result of ad-hoc decisions taken by the Government. The explicitly stated reasons for many such Public Enterprises are that corporate form would enable the departmental functions to be performed more expeditiously and supplementary funds would be available from financial institutions resulting in less burden on state budget.

A list of Public Enterprises, according to their functions,

is given at Annexure- II. The investment, profit and loss, establishment cost for all the Public Enterprises for last four years are given at Annexure- III. The total investment of the State Government in these enterprises up to 31.3.86 was to the tune of Rs. 2289.00 crores. The rate of growth in the investment in the SLPEs is given in Table- 4.2. Most of them have not been able to show profits. The total cumulative loss stands at Rs. 505.8 crores and profits earned amount to Rs. 33.4 crores. The net loss is Rs. 472.4 crores Bihar State Electricity Board, and Bihar State Road Transport Corporation together account for major portion of the losses. For the rest major loss incurring enterprises are in manufacturing sector, water development i.e. irrigation corporation and construction corporation. Public Enterprises rendering financial services like Bihar State Financial Corporation, Bihar State Credit and Investment Corporation etc. are making profit. Other corporations which are making profit are Forest Development Corporation, Warehousing Corporation etc. Bureau of Public Enterprises has classified the Public Enterprises into five categories according to their functions i.e. manufacturing, trading and service enter- prises, construction and contracting, promotional/ regulatory Boards/authorities, and financial services.

Prior to the First Plan, the State had nationalised certain selected road routes[1]. Initially, the bus services were run on departmental basis. This seems to be the only example of the departmentally organised economic activity. With the formation of the Bihar State Road Transport Corporation in 1959 the departmental form of organisation had to face its extinction from the SLPEs. In 1984-85, out of 49 SLPEs, 20 units were Statutory Corporations/Boards and 29 undertakings had been government companies. During the Fourth, Fifth and Sixth Plan periods, a large number of the SLPEs were setup in the form of government companies. As a matter of fact, there was no change in the number of statutory corporations/boards. During 1977-78 to 1984-85 the authorities and boards were set up to industrialise certain local areas and develop a few urban areas in the planned manner. The autonomous Industrial Area Development Authorities were set up at Bokaro, Jamshedpur, Ranchi, Patna, Muzaffarpur and Darbhanga. Their basic function is to develop infrastructural facilities and make them available to small enterpreneurs at concessional rates. These authorities are located in close proximity of major core sector projects such as Heavy Engineering Corporation, Bokaro Steel and the Tata Engineering and locomotive Works. Three Regional Development Authorities were set up at Patna, Ranchi and Muzaffarpur. These authorities are responsible for an integrated development of the three urban areas. The Industrial Development Authorities were set up under the Bihar Industrial Area Development Authority Ordinance, 1972. The ordinance was replaced later by an Act in 1974. The three Urban Regional Development Authorities were also established under the Bihar Regional Development Authority (earlier Ordinance) Act, 1974. The basic reason behind organising these activities in the form of autonomous authorities/boards was to recognise their special role and equip them accordingly with special status. This apart, a large number of organisations were, however, set up in the form of government companies. One of the motivations for setting up the SLPEs in this form was to secure institutional finance, provide them operational freedom in the day-to-day management and apply to them the same provisions as applicable to similar enterprises in the private sector. Table-4.3 shows the organisational structure of the SLPEs.

The Boards in majority of the cases are policy ones, jampacked by officials and politicians. The professionals and other groups have not found any worthwhile representation.

The size has varied from a minimum of 6 to 15. In most of the cases, the two offices of the Chairman and Managing Director have been separated. The Bihar Government appointed Chairmen for 36 enterprises and Chairmen-cum-Managing Directors for 13 enterprises. The MLAs, MPs, Ministers and other politicians manned the post of Chairman in the case of 36 enterprises. Among the officials, Commissioners and Secretaries and the officers of the Bihar Provincial Services manned the posts of 11 CMDs. Eleven SLPEs had appointed Vice-Chairman too. The tenure of the board members including Managing Directors, Chairman and Vice-Chairman was very short and less than two years in most cases. In certain cases, the tenure of Managing Directors was cut short to less than one year. Table-4.4 provides details about the representative character of the Chairman in the Boards of SLPEs.

On an investment of Rs. 2089.11 crores as on March 31,1985 the SLPEs had accumulated a loss of Rs. 263.63 crores. In none of the years between 1977-78 and 1984-85, these enterprises earned net profits higher than the net losses incurred. As a result, the accumulated losses shot up from Rs. 131.11 crores in 1977-78 to Rs. 263.63 crores in 1984-85. The SLPEs in all the functional categories taken together incurred net losses in 1984-85. A detailed break-up, however, reveals that the enterprises engaged in the field of financial services were exception. Annexure-II presents the consolidated data on investment and returns.

The salient features of the financial performance of the SLPEs are as follows -

(i) The investments have been increasing but the net worth of SLPEs has been decreasing.

(ii) The turnover of capital employed is very low and shows a declining trend. The turnover rate was 0.26 in 1982-83 and 0.21 in 1984-85.

(iii) The debt-equity ratio in these enterprises is very high. In 1984-85 it was 10:1.

(iv) The Bihar State Electricity Board and Bihar State Road Transport Corporation have two-thirds of the investment and contribute to more than half of the total losses incurred by the SLPEs.

(v) The cost structure is inconducive and the cost of sales was higher than the final prices in the case of 18 SLPEs in 1984-85. Some of these enterprises suffered even cash losses.

The causes of unsatisfactory financial performance as contained in the Annual Report on the Working of State Public Undertakings have been depicted in Table-4.5.

An analysis of Table-4.5 reveals that the problems faced are:

(i) very elementary in nature

(ii) not variegated, and

(iii) further both the managements of these enterprises and the State Government lack commitment to run these units as enterprises. Whereas the "managements" have failed to demonstrate any innovativeness to encounter the operational and policy problems, the Government appears to have adopted the attitude of indifference to the post-natal problems of these enterprises.

The control structuring including internal and external control systems is not much different in Bihar as compared to the other States. The accounting process is in a mess. In the case of many SLPEs annual accounts have not been finalised for over five years and more. Out of 49 SLPEs 11 had this distinction in 1984-85.

One distinguishing feature of the Governmental control of these enterprises is the creation of Bureau of Public Enterprise in the year 19763. The Bureau was set up to coordinate, monitor and control the working of the SLPEs. The Bureau was initially put under the charge of the Commissioner, Institutional Finance. Later on in October 1978 a separate post of the Chairman was created for the Bureau. The Commissioner of the Bureau was also designated as Ex-Officio Principal Secretary of the Department of Finance. To strengthen the Bureau and make its working more effective in January 1980 the post of the Chairman of the Bureau was upgraded as equivalent to the post of Chief Secretary, Government of Bihar and Secretary to the Government of India. Nowhere such a status has been provided to the chief of a nodal agency for the SLPEs in the country. The Bureau has made efforts to professionalise the managerial personnel in the SLPEs by way of organising the management development and training programmes. In this endeavour it has taken the assistance of the management and professional institutions. The Government of Bihar entrusted to the Bureau the task of recruiting Class-I and Class-II employees for the SLPEs. The Bureau has been able to attract technocrats and professionals. It has taken steps to help the SLPEs in the preparation and finalisation of their accounts. The Bureau has undertaken evaluation studies of some SLPEs. In its indepth studies it has observed that wasteful and unproductive expenditure has affected the financial performance of the SLPEs. It has observed that frequent shifting of the Managing Directors had also contributed to their low performance. A high level committee was constituted by the Bureau at the behest of the Cabinet to study the management problems of the SLPEs. On the recommendations of the Committee, the Bureau fixed a tenure of three years for the Managing Directors and to minimise the frequent rifts between Bureau Chairman and Managing

Director and define roles and responsibilities of the non-official chairman and vice-chairman.

A review of the work of the Bureau indicates that its achievement have fallen short of expectations. Though it has been provided a very high status. It has not pushed forward its programmes effectively. In the case of some SLPEs. The Managing Directors were changed 4 to 5 times in a period of two years. The problem of deputationists in some SLPEs continues to be critical. The Bihar State Tourism Development Corporation had more than 50 per cent of its employees drawn on deputation. The Bihar State Hydro Electric Development Corporation. Patna Industrial Regional Development Authority and Bihar State Seeds Corporation could be cited as other examples where deputationists were on the rolls in a sizeable number. An important activity of the Bureau is the preparation of annual reports on the working of State Undertakings. The report is sketchy both in macro and micro terms and it contains inadequate information pertaining to the different facets of the working of the SLPEs and does not bring out the salient features of the working of these enterprises. Moreover, the contents of the report have changed from year to year and the consistency in presentation is conspicuous by its absence.

It is not always fair to compare the profit of Public Enterprises with that of their private counterparts. Public Enterprises have multiple objectives and social responsibilities not only for economic growth but also for an equitable distribution of economic benefits. While it is true that profit motive cannot be the sole or even the principal objective of public undertakings, it is a fallacy to ever that it is of no relevance. Denial of relevance of profit inheres a serious danger in that it may act as a cover for organisational deficiencies and weaken the will to achieve optional performance. Public Enterprises have to ensure generation of internal resources not only for replacement and renewal of their requirements of plant and machinery as also for expansion and future growth so as to minimise their dependence on the State Exchequer, and to generate additional resources for all economic development of the state.

Bureau of Public Enterprises has been also to identify major problems facing Public Enterprises in Bihar.

(a) *A lack of clarity in objectives*--An analysis of Public Enterprises indicates that there is no clear cut definition of objectives or prioritisation of objectives which enterprises are expected to fulfill. The commercial and social objectives are not clearly defined in terms of tasks which can be evaluated in financial terms.

(b) *Lack of motivation of Personnel*--The greatest challenge facing the Public Enterprises of Bihar is lack of motivation of both managerial personnel and workers. There is need to improve the work culture.

The nexus between the benefits enjoyed by the Public Enterprises employees and the Government employees is often viewed so closely that it renders difficult for the state itself (let alone the Public Enterprises) to allow any degree of functional freedom in the system in respect of Public Enterprises employees.

The work culture of the State Government (which is far from healthy) has unfortunately permeated down to Public Enterprises.

(c) *Overmanning*--Another problem confronting the larger State Public Enterprises is the problem of overmanning. Disproportionate emphasis on provision of job by industries often lead to over-employment.

Redundancy of manpower in any organisation demoralises the work force and undermines work ethic. Often action plan to reduce overstaffing, redeployment of manpower evokes resistance from trade unions and political executives.

(d) *The Management Policy*--The choice of top management is of crucial importance for the successful includes the Board of Directors and the Managing Director.

As regards the post of Chief Executives of Public Enterprises, there is no well recognised policy regarding either the appointment of the tenure. Chief Executives of Public Enterprises are with a few exceptions, drawn from Civil Service. In Bihar Public Enterprises average tenure of Chief Executives is 11 months. In some cases the Chief Executives had a very short period of less than three months.

An analysis of the composition of the Board of Directors of Public Enterprises reveals that 33% of Board comprised of public figures -57% official and only 10% come from professional experts.

(e) *Low Technology*--State Public Enterprises owing to their small size and financial constraints find it difficult to upgrade their technology resulting in difficulties in selling their product. In the fast changing industrial scene it is important that Public Enterprises modernise and wherever necessary diversify their products in order to make them competitive in the market.

(f) *Constraints in decision making*--There are quite a few departments/agencies which look after Public Enterprises e.g. Administrative Department, Finance Department, Planning Department, Bureau of Public Enterprises etc. Many important decision of Public Enterprises require government approval as a result of which Public Enterprises find it difficult to take timely decisions.

Bureau of Public Enterprises has been engaged in fixing annual targets of performance for each enterprise to ensure a realistic operational programme to achieve twin objectives laid down by Government for Public Enterprises i.e. to increase efficiency and productivity and to ensure generation of surplus for development. This exercise is carried out in consultation with the administrative department and the Public Enterprise.

The performance is closely monitored by a group under the Chairmanship of Chairman, Bureau of Public Enterprise, Principal Secretary to Government of the administrative department, Secretary of the Department, Finance Secretary, Planning Secretary and Managing Director. This high powered group also helps in sorting out problems of Public Enterprises.

Another important function carried out by the Bureau of Public Enterprise is the recruitment of executives for Public Enterprises. The management development programmes like training etc. are organised by the Bureau of Public Enterprise.

The need of the hour appears to be to professionalise these Public Enterprises and enable them to function freely in the framework of agreed Action Plans with specific and clear objectives. There is also a pressing necessity to make a concerted effort to bring about an amaleoroation in the work-culture of the state level enterprises, which is closely linked with the politico-administrative culture in which we are functioning at present.

TABLE 4.1

Growth in Number of SLPEs in Bihar

Year	*No. of PEs*
1969-70	8
1970-71	8
1971-72	14
1972-73	18
1973-74	25
1974-75	36
1975-76	38
1976-77	38
1977-78	42
1978-79	42
1979-80	44
1980-81	44
1981-82	45
1982-83	46
1983-84	49
1984-85	49
1985-86	49

TABLE 4.2

Investment in SLPEs of Bihar

Year	*No. of enterprises*	*Total investment (Rs. in crores)*	*Preceding Year growth*
1977-78	42	796.11	- -
1978-79	42	1040.16	30.65
1979-80	44	1232.57	18.50
1980-81	44	1320.93	7.20
1981-82	45	1477.78	11.87
1982-83	46	1746.34	18.18
1983-84	49	1689.29	-3.23
1984-85	49	2069.11	23.60

TABLE 4.3

Organisation Structure of SLPEs in Bihar

Year	*Statutory Corporation form*	*Autonomous Authorities and boards*	*Company form*	*Total*
1969-70	4	- -	4	8
1970-71	4	- -	4	8
1971-72	6	2	6	14
1972-73	6	4	8	18
1973-74	7	4	14	25
1974-75	8	8	20	36
1975-76	8	8	22	38
1976-77	8	8	22	38
1977-78	9	9	24	42
1978-79	9	9	24	42
1979-80	9	9	26	44
1980-81	9	9	26	44
1981-82	9	9	27	45
1982-83	9	10	27	46
1983-84	8	13	28	49
1984-85	8	13	28	49

TABLE 4.4

Representative Character of Chairman in SLPEs of Bihar in 1984-85

Sl. No.	*Administrative Department*	*Total*	*M.L.A's/ M.Ps*	*Minister*	*Other active politicians*	*Chairman cum M.D.*	*Commi ssioner & Secretary*	*Other Bureau-crats*	*Others*	*Vice Chair-man*
1	Industries	17	5	-	4	3	3	2	1	3
2	Sugarcans	1	-	-	-	1	-	-	-	1
3.	Agriculture	4	1	-	1	-	2	-	-	-
4.	Minor Irrigation	2	1	-	-	1	-	-	-	-
5.	Animal Husbandry	2	1	-	-	-	-	-	-	1
6.	Cooperation	1	-	-	-	1	-	-	-	-
7.	Food & Civil Supplies	1	-	-	-	1	-	-	-	-
8.	Education	1	-	-	-	-	1	-	-	1
9.	Forestry	1	-	1	-	-	-	-	-	-
10.	Irrigation	1	1	-	-	-	-	-	-	1
11.	Power	2	-	-	-	2	-	-	-	-
12.	Mining	1	-	-	1	-	-	-	-	1
13.	Home	2	1	-	-	-	-	1	-	-
14.	Rural Development	1	1	-	-	-	-	-	-	1
15.	Urban Development	7	-	5	1	1	-	-	-	-
16.	Road & Transport	2	1	-	1	1	-	-	-	2
17.	Public Health Engineering	2	-	-	-	1	-	-	-	-
18.	Tourism Development	1	-	-	-	1	-	-	-	-
		49	12	6	8	13	6	3	1	11

TABLE 4.5

Causes of Low Financial Performance of SLPEs in Bihar--1984-85

Sl. No.	*Causes*	*No. of SLPEs*
1.	Inadequate supply of inputs	6
2.	Obsolete machinery	2
3.	Lack of suitable personnel	3
4.	Lack of working capital	8
5.	Overstaffing	6
6.	Lack of long term finance	8
7.	Government attitude	6
8.	Realisation of debts	2
9.	Marketing	2
10.	Natural calamities	1
11.	Organisation Development including management	4
12.	Frequent change of Managing Directors	1
13.	Deputationists	4
14.	Non-Remunerative prices	1

Status of SLPEs in Bihar

The profile of SLPEs of Bihar is given in Table 4.6

TABLE 4.6

Status of SLPEs in Bihar

(Rs. in crore)

Bihar

Items	*1998-99*	*1999-00*	*2000-01*	*2001-02*	*2002-03*	*2003-04*
	Years					
1. Total no. of SLPEs	50	53	54	54	54	54
2. No.of Working SLPEs	17	22	18	21	21	20
3. No.of Non-Working SLPEs	33	31	32	33	33	34
(i) Under liquidation	3	2	3			
(ii) Under Closure	30	1				
(iii) Under Merger						
(iv) Others		28	29			
4. Total Equity	421.36	605.60	610.23	458.51	458.51	457.73
5. Total Debt	1479.87	1778.80	7558.39	8017.86	8123.26	5977.41
6. Total Investment	1901.23	2384.40	8168.62	8476.37	8581.73	6435.14
7. No.of Profit making enterprises	6	6	8	8	8	10
8. No.of Loss making enterprises	39	39		13	13	10
9. Net Profit/Loss	-84.67	-580.53		-1127.32	-1127.32	1031.82
10. Accumulated Loss(-)/Profit	-413.71	-2385.93		-	-9668.65	-9610.14

(*Source:* Reports of the Comptroller and Auditor General of India (Commercial), on Bihar for 1998-99 to 2003-04)

ANNEXURE - I

GROWTH OF NUMBER OF SLPEs IN BIHAR

Sl. No	*Name of Public Enterprise*	*Name of Administrative Department*	*Year of*	*Nature of Origin*
1.	Bihar State Industries Development Corporation	Industries Department	1960	Companies Act 1956
2.	Bihar State Leather Development Corporation	-do-	1974	-do-
3.	Bihar State Electronics Development Corporation	-do-	1976	-do-
4.	Bihar State Textile Corporation	-do-	1978	-do-
5.	Bihar State Pharmaceutical and Chemical Dev. Corporation	-do-	1978	-do-
6.	Bihar State Agro Industries Dev. Corporation	Agriculture Department	1966	-do-
7.	Bihar State Fruit and Vegetable Dev. Corpn.	-do-	1980	-do-
8.	Bihar State Dairy Corporation	Animal Husbandry Deptt.	1972	-do-
9.	Bihar State Sugar Corporation	Cane Department	1974	-do-
10.	Bihar State Khadi Board	Industries Department	1956	Bihar Khadi and village Industries Act 1956.
11.	Bihar State Small Industries Crop.	-do-	1961	Companies Act 1956
12.	Bihar State Handloom and Handicraft Corporation	-do-	1974	-do-
13.	Bihar State Agriculture Marketing Board	Agriculture Department	1972	Bihar Raj Agriculture Uppag.
14.	Bihar State Forest Dev. Corp.	Forest & Folluation Dept.	1975	Companies Act 1956
15.	Bihar State Export Corpn.	Industries Department	1974	-do-
16.	Bihar State Beej Corp.	Agriculture Department	1978	-do-
17.	Bihar State Matsya Beej Vikas Nigam	Animal Husbandry Deptt.	1980	-do-
18.	Bihar State Warehousing Corpn.	Cooperative Deptt.	1957	The Warehousing Corporation Act. 1956

19.	Bihar State Tourism Dev. Corpn.	Tourism Department	1980	Companies Act, 1956
20	Bihar State Road Transport Corpn.	Transport Department	1959	Road Transport Corpn. Act.
21	Bihar State Food and Civil Supply Corporation	Food Supply and Commerce Department	1973	Companies Act, 1956
22	Bihar State Text Book Publishing Corporation	Education Department	1965	-do-
23	Bihar State Construction Corpn.	Irrigation Department	1974	-do-
24	Bihar State Min. Dev. Corpn.	Mines and Geology	1972	-do-
25	Bihar State Housing Board	Urban Development and Housing Department	1972	Bihar State Housing Board ordinance, 1972
26	Bihar State Pool Nirman Nigam	Road Construction Department	1973	Companies Act, 1956
27	Bihar State Police Building Construction Corpn.	Home (Special) Department	1975	-do-
28	Bihar State Electricity Board	Electricity Department	1958	Indian Electric Supply Act, 1956
29	Bihar State Hydro Electricity Corpn.	Electricity Department	1962	Companies Act, 1956
30	Bihar State Water Dev. Corpn.	Minor Irrigation Department	1973	-do-
31	Bihar State Lift Irrigation Corpn.	-do-	1975	-do-
32	Bihar State Industrial Area Dev. Authority	Industries Department	1973	Bihar Industrial Area Dev. Auth-Ority Act, 1974
33	Bokaro Industrial Area Development Authority	-do-	1972	-do-
34	Ranchi Industrial Area Development Authority	-do	1973	-do
35	Adityapur Industrial Area Development Authority	Industrial Department	1972	Bihar Industrial Area Dev. Authority Act, 1974
36	North Bihar Industrial Area Development Authority	-do-	1975	-do-
37	Darbhanga Industrial Development Authority	-do-	1972	-do-
38	Patna Regional Development Authority	Urban Development and Housing Department	1975	Bihar Regional Development Authority Ordinance (now Act 1974)

39	Ranchi Regional Dev. Authority	-do-	1975	-do-
40	Muzaffarpur Regional Development Authority	-do-	1973	-do-
41	Darbhanga Regional Development Authority	-do-	1983	Bihar Regional Development Authority Ordinance, 1981
42	Gaya Regional Dev. Authority	-do-	1983	-do-
43	Bihar State Pollution Board	Forest & Pollution Deptt.	1974	Pollution Control Act, 1974
44	Bihar State Water and Severage Board	P. II. Department	1979	
45	Bihar State Financial Corp.	Industries Department	1954	Bihar Raj Financial Corp. Act, 1954
46	Bihar State Credit and Investment Corporation	-do-	1975	Companies Act, 1956
47	Bihar Panchayati Raj Finance Corporation	Rural Development Deptt.	1974	-do-
48	Bihar State Film Development and Finance Corporation	Industries Department	1983	-do-
49	Bihar State Minority Finance Corporation	Home (Special) Deptt.	1983	-do-

ANNEXURE -II

LIST OF PUBLIC ENTERPRISES IN BIHAR

S. No.	*Name of Public Undertaking*
	Established between 1950-1959
1.	Bihar State Khadi Board
2.	Bihar State Warehousing Corporation
3.	Bihar State Road Transport Corporation
4.	Bihar State Electricity Board
5.	Bihar State Financial Corporation
	Established between 1960- 1969
1.	Bihar State Industrial Development Corporation
2.	Bihar State Agro Industries Dev. Corporation
3.	Bihar State Small Industries Corp.
4.	Bihar State Text Book Publishing Corp.
	Established between 1970-1979
1.	Bihar State Leather Dev. Corp.
2.	Bihar State Electronics Dev. Corporation
3.	Bihar State Textile Corp.
4.	Bihar State Pharmaceutical and Chemical Dev. Corp.
5.	Bihar State Dairy Corporation
6.	Bihar State Sugar Corp.
7.	Bihar State Handloom and Handicraft Corp.
8.	Bihar State Agricultural Marketing Board
9.	Bihar State Forest Dev. Corp.
10.	Bihar State Export Corp.
11.	Bihar State Beej Dev. Corp.
12.	Bihar State Food & Civil Supplies Corp.
13.	Bihar State Construction Corp.
14.	Bihar State Mineral Dev. Corp.
15.	Bihar State Housing Board
16.	Bihar State Pul Nirman Nigam
17.	Bihar State Police Building Construction Corp.

18. Bihar State Water Dev. Corp.
19. Bihar State Lift Irrigation Corp.
20. Patna Industrial Area Dev. Authority
21. Bokaro Industrial Area Development Authority
22. Ranchi Industrial Area Development Authority
23. Adityapur Industrial Area Dev. Authority
24. North Bihar Industrial Area Dev. Authority
25 Darbhanga Industrial Area Dev. Authority
26 Patna Regional Development Authority
27 Ranchi Regional Development Authority
28 Muzaffarpur Regional Development Authority
29 Darbhanga Regional Development Authority
30 Bihar State Pollution Board
31 Bihar State Sewerage Board
32 Bihar State Credit & Investment Corp. Ltd.,
33 Bihar Panchayati Raj Finance Corp. Ltd.,

Established between 1980-1987

1. Bihar State Fruits & Vegetable Dev. Corp. Ltd.
2. Bihar State Matsya Beej Vikas Nigam
3. Bihar State Tourism Dev. Corp.
4. Bihar Hydro-Electricity Corpn.
5. Gaya Regional Dev. Authority
6. Darbhanga Regional Dev. Authority
7. Bihar State Film Dev. Corporation
8. Bihar State Minority Finance Corporation

ANNEXURE - III

INVESTMENT PATTERNS IN SLPES

Sl.No. Enterprise	Name of Public Enterprise	Investment			
		March '83	March '84	March '85	March '86
GROUP 'A' PRODUCTION ORIENTED ENTERPRISES					
1.	B.S. Industrial Dev. Corp. Ltd.	2421.1	2731.1	3056.1	3697.1
2.	B.S Leather Dev. Corp. Ltd.	610.1	695.1	860.1	1250.1
3.	B.S. Finished Leather Ltd.	730.9	933.9	967.5	1099.5
4.	B.S. Electronic Dev. Corp. Ltd.	144.1	224.1	295.1	416.1
5.	B.S. Sugar Corp. Ltd.	3013.1	4121.1	5418.1	7455.1
6.	B.S. Chemical & Pharmaceutical Corp. Ltd.	443.1	711.4	953.4	1236.1
7.	B.S. Fruit & Vegitable Corp. Ltd.	53.1	87.1	154.1	233.1
8.	B.S. Agro Industries Corp. Ltd.	882.1	962.1	142.1	1294.1
9.	B.S Dairy Dev. Corp. Ltd.	764.1	903.1	907.6	918.6
10.	B.S Textile Corp. Ltd.	117.1	150.1	285.1	259.7
	Total	9178.1	11519.1	13039.2	17839.5
GROUP 'B' TRADING & SERVICE ENTERPRISES					
11.	B.S. Small Industries Dev. Corp. Ltd.	1889.7	1160.8	1238.2	1385.4
12.	B.S. Handloom & Handicraft Corp. Ltd.	705.1	724.1	835.1	889.1
13.	B.S. Forest Dev. Corp. Ltd.	170.4	195.9	225.2	349.5
14	B.S. Export Corp. Ltd.	72.5	87.5	102.5	121.5
15	B.S. Seeds Dev. Corp. Ltd.	453.9	530.5	942.6	1186.1
16.	B.S. Fishery Dev. Corp. Ltd.	55.1	55.1	87.5	154.6
17.	B.S. Warehousing Corp. Ltd.	143.6	151.5	147.5	12.05
18.	B.S. Tourism Dev. Corp. Ltd.	57.1	122.1	147.4	168.9
19.	B.S. Raj Transport Corp. Ltd.	5344.1	5784.1	7005.1	8363.1
20.	B.S. Food & Civil Supplies Dev. Corp.	3341.1	3341.1	4895.6	4710.9
21	B.S. Textbook & Publishing Dev. Corp. Ltd.	52.1	48.1	48.1	48.1
	TOTAL 'B'	12284.7	12200.1	15675.2	17497.7
GROUP 'C' CONSTRUCTION & CONSTRUCTION ENTERPRISES					
22.	B.S. Construction Corp. Ltd.	700.1	700.1	700.1	700.1
23.	B.S. Mineral Development Corp. Ltd.	223.1	248.1	275.1	285.1

24.	B.S. Bridge Construction Corp. Ltd.	150.1	150.1	150.1	150.1
25.	B.S. Hydroelectric Dev. Corp. Ltd.	80.1	780.1	1230.1	2230.1
26.	B.S. Polic Bldg. Construction Corp. Ltd.	2040.1	2772.1	2889.6	4086.9
27.	B.S. Electricity Board	108807.1	122550.1	141386.1	162885.1
28.	B.S. Water Development Corp. Ltd.	7220.7	7822.2	8629.4	9115.9
29.	B.S. Hill Area Lift Irrigation Corp. Ltd.	950.8	1167.9	1426.8	1945.4
	TOTAL 'C'	120172.1	136191.0	156687.3	181498.7
GROUP 'E' FINANCIAL SERVICE ENTERPRISES					
30	B.S. Financial Corp. Ltd.	6423.1	1983.1	729.1	8556.1
31	B.S. Credit & Investment Corp. Ltd.	1225.9	1815.4	2248.9	2835.1
32	B.S. Panchaity Raj Finance Corp. Ltd.	417.4	494.8	519.9	100.1
33	B.S. Minority Finance Corp. Ltd.		100.1	100.1	100.1
34	B.S. Filim Dev. & Finance Corp. Ld.	2.1	5.1	5.1	15.1
	TOTAL 'E'	8068.5	4398.5	9903.1	12047.3
	SUB-TOTALS				
	GROUP 'A'	9178.8	11519.1	13039.2	17839.5
	GROUP 'B'	12284.7	12200.8	15675.2	17497.7
	GROUP 'C'	120172.1	136191.0	156687.3	181498.7
	GROUP 'E'	8068.5	4398.5	9903.1	12047.3
	GRAND TOTAL	14974.1	164309.4	195304.8	228883.2

Sl.No. Enter prise	*Name of Public*	*Investment*			
		March '83	*March '84*	*March '85*	*March '86*
1.	B.S. Industrial Dev. Corp. Ltd.	-100.1	-151.8	-186.1	-
2.	B.S. Leather Dev. Corp. Ltd.	-34.1	-68.1	-65.1	-90.1
3.	B.S. Finished Leathers Ltd.	-63.7	-149.4	-172.6	-181.5
4.	B.S. Electronics Dev. Corp. Ltd.	-2.3	-3.5	-1.5	-5.1
5.	B.S. Sugar Corp. Ltd.	-1403.1	-935.7	-617.1	-528.1
6.	B.S. Chemical & Pharmaceutical Dev. Corp. Ltd.	-15.5	-16.2	-13.2	-18.4
7.	B.S. Fruit & Vegitable Dev. Corp. Ltd.	-0.3	-2.9	-8.1	-19.6
8.	B.S. Agro Industries Dev. Corp.	-125.1	-132.1	-138.1	-128.1
9.	B.S. Dairty Corp. Ltd.	-32.1	-42.1	-141.4	-34.8
10.	B.S. Textile Corp. Ltd.	-1.4	-0.7	-1.4	-3.2
	TOTAL 'A'	1800.7	-1501.1	-1344.6	-1230.0

GROUP 'B' TRADING & SERVICE ENTERPRISES					
11.	B.S. Small Industries Dev. Corp. Ltd.	-115.7	-116.8	-96.3	-136.
12.	B.S. Handloom & Handicraft Corp. Ltd.	1.1	0.4	0.5	-0.3
13.	B.S. Forest Dev. Corp. Ltd.	8.2	5.8	9.6	13.4
14.	B.S. Export Corp. Ltd.	3.1	1.1	14.1	-8.6
15.	B.S. Seeds Dev. Corp. Ltd.	-58.2	4.3	10.8	-49.1
16.	B.S. Fishery Seeds Dev. Corp. Ltd.	-	-	-	-
17.	B.S. Warehouse Corp. Ltd.	21.7	32.9	39.9	104.2
18.	B.S. Tourism Dev. Corp. Ltd.	-9.8	-4.1	-4.1	-4.1
19.	B.S. Raj Transport Corp. Ltd.	-1102.7	-1209.9	-1559.1	-1606.1
20	B.S. Food & Civil Supply Corp. Ltd.	60.9	86.2	-635.1	-581.1
21.	B.S. Textbook & Publishing Corp.	124.8	41.1	-39.7	-12.3
	TOTAL 'B'	-1066.6	-1159.0	-2277.4	-2280.0
GROUP 'C' CONSTRUCTION & CONSTRUCTING ENTERPRISES					
22	B.S. Construction Corp. Ltd.	-173.6	1.1	-195.9	
23	B.S. Mineral Dev. Corp. Ltd.	-11.3	-24.1	-20.4	0.1
24	B.S. Bridge Construction Corp. Ltd.	-25.1	-27.1	-10.1	-15.9
25	B.S. Police Building Construction Corp.	6.9	-15.3	-45.5	12.3
26	B.S. Electricity Board	-903.3	-1266.7	-963.7	-11111.0
27	B.S. Hydroelectric Power Dev. Corp. Ltd.	-13.1	-27.2	-52.2	-65.9
28	B.S. Water Dev. Corp. Ltd.	-658.1	-799.1	-400.1	-905.6
29	B.S. Hill Area Lift Irrigation Corp.	-3.9	-53.3	-58.2	
	TOTAL 'C'	25.1	-2211.7	1725.9	13087.0
GROUP 'E' FINANCIAL SERVICE ENTERPRISES					
30	B.S. Financial Corp. Ltd.	195.1	218.2	232.1	245.1
31	B.S. Credit & Investment Corp. Ltd.	-5.6	9.8	146.2	-37.1
32	B.S. Panchayati Raj Finance Corp. Ld. 0.3	0.2	2.4	5.1	
33	B.S. Minority Corp. Ltd.				
34	B.S. Film Dev. & Finance Corp. Ltd.				
	TOTAL 'E'	134.8	228.2	300.7	213.1
	SUB-TOTAL				
	GROUP 'A'	-1900.7	-1501.1	-1344.6	-1232.0
	GROUP 'B'	-1066.6	-1155.0	-2277.4	-2280.0
	GROUP 'C'	25.1	-2211.7	-1725.9	-3087.0
	GROUP 'E'	184.8	228.2	380.7	213.1
	GRAND TOTAL	-2657.4	-4643.6	-4967.2	-16391.9

5

Overview of Performance of Public Sector Enterprises of Government of Gujarat

*M.B.G. Tilak**

This paper attempts to analyse the growth, pattern of Public Enterprise system in Gujarat, the investment structure made into the Public Sector Enterprises system, the financial performance, analysis of profit/loss making enterprises, management patterns, social obligations, problems faced by the enterprises, etc.

Introduction

The public enterprises system undoubtedly has been universally accepted as an effective vehicle of transformation of economic development at a speedier rate for our country. Recognising this vital aspect, the Government of Gujarat have established a number of public sector enterprises (PSEs). As on 31st March 1983, the Gujarat Government owns about 50 PEs comprising of 38 Government companies and 12 Statutory Undertakings.

Mainly the State Sector Enterprises in Gujarat consists of two categories: (a) Government companies formed under the Companies Act, 1956; (b) the Statutory Undertakings performing the commercial or quasi-commercial functions under different statutes. Besides the above, there are a number of departmental undertakings, autonomous bodies registered under the Registration of Societies Act, but they are not considered in this paper.

Growth Pattern

There is a considerable growth of Public Enterprise system and proliferation of the same into different segments of society since its inception. A glance of the Table-5.1 indicates that there is a sharp increase in the growth of Public Enterprises commensurate with the investment made into the sector which could be viewed from Table-5.2. As on 31st March 1981 the total resources diverted into the Public Sector Enterprises stream tends to be of the order of Rs. 308.31 crores. It is obvious from Table 5.2 that the investment made by the State Government in Public Enterprises increased from Rs. 606.83 crores on 31st March 1983 to Rs. 404.73 crores as on 31st March 1984, indicating an average annual increase of 32.87%. The total resources at the disposal of these Public Enterprises increased from Rs. 1443.18 crores as on 31st March 1981 to Rs. 3008.31 crores as on 31st March 1984 indicating an average annual increase of 27.11%. Perhaps the phenomenal increase in the resources invested by the State Government as well as

TABLE 5.1

Date	*Number of Government Companies*	*Number of Statutory Undertakings*	*Total number of Public Enterprise*
1	2	3	4
31-3-80	32	11	43
31-3-81	35	11	46
31-3-82	37	11	48
31-3-83	38	12	50
31-3-84	38	12	50

by other agencies is an indication of efforts taken by the Government in achieving the required amount of development through the Public Enterprise system in the pursuit of transforming its policies into action for the betterment of the public.

TABLE 5.2

Date	*Total Investment by State Government (Rs. in crores)*	*Total Resources (Rs. in crores)*	*Percentage of State Government Investment to total resources*
1	2	3	4
31-3-80	606.83	1443.18	42.05
31-3-81	756.30 (24.63)	1758.73 (21.86)	43.00
31-3-82	865.76 (14.47)	2153.14 (22.77)	40.10
31-3-83	1190-00 (37.45)	2726.27 (26.27)	43.65
31-3-84	1404.72 (18.04)	3008.31 (10.35)	46.69

Note: 1. Figures in brackets denote percentage increase over previous year.

2. Figures in respect of Gujarat State Civil Supplies Corporation Limited and Gujarat Scheduled Castes Economic Development Corporation Limited for 31-3-82, 31-3-83 and 31-3-84 and Gujarat Water Supply and Sewerage Board for 31-3-83 and 31-3-84 have not been included as the same are not available.

Financial Position

The financial performance in respect of these public sector Enterprises in the State has considerably improved since 1980-81 as could be viewed from Table-5.3. It is obvious from the above data that the turnover/revenue of all Public Enterprises has sharply increased from Rs. 526.08 crores in 1980-81 to Rs. 1100.33 crores in 1983-84. Similarly, the percentage of turnover/revenue to capital employed which remained at 36.40 during the year 1980-81 has sharply increased to 59.77 in the year 1983-84. There is also substantial improvement in the percentage of return on the capital made, which could be viewed from column 7 of the Table-5.3. Similarly, the profitability also has increased considerably. Till the year

TABLE 5.3

Parameter	*1980-81*	*1981-82*	*1982-83*	*1983-84*
Net Worth*	154.46	174.87	244.84	329.36
Capital Employed*	1445.45	1286.87	1456.11	1684.65
Turnover total Income*	526.08	757.58	869.77	1010.33
Return on Capital Employed*	13.31	54.04	91.20	123.46
Net Profit After Income Tax*	-67.70	-39.82	-9.05	12.03
Percentage of turnover on capital employed	36.40	58.86	59.73	59.97
Percentage of return on capital employed	0.92	4.19	6.26	7.32
Percentage of net profit after income tax on net worth	-44.03	-22.90	-3.92	3.84

* Rs. in crore

TABLE-5.4(A)

Sl. No.	*Name of the Enterprise*	*Profit during 1983-84 (Rs. in Lakhs)*	*Result of 1982-83 Profit (+) Loss (-)*
1.	Gujarat Agro Industries Corporation Ltd.	70.80	
2.	Gujarat Communications and Electronics Ltd.	74.40	(+) 54.41
3.	Gujarat Dairy Development Corporation Ltd.	15.64	27.80
4.	Gujarat Industrial Investment Corporation Ltd.	85.52	112.72
5.	Gujarat Mineral Development Corporation Ltd.	539.27	222.47
6.	Gujarat Sheep and Wool Development Corporation Ltd.	0.55	10.20
7.	Gujarat Small Industries Corporation Ltd.	38.00	0.99
8.	Gujarat State Construction Corporation Ltd.	14.15	(-)243.65
9.	Gujarat State Export Corporation Ltd.	0.14	103.83
10.	Gujarat State Handloom Development Corporation	9.82	(-)3.97

1982-83 the aggregate results of all Public Enterprises were showing losses, while in the year 1983-84 the aggregate results of all Public Enterprises showed a net profit of Rs. 12.03 crores. The aggregate losses after taxation of all Public Enterprises show of the order of Rs. 67.70 crores during the year 1980-81, Rs. 39.82 crores during the year 1981-82 and Rs. 9.05 crores during the year 1982-83, while in the year 1983-84 the aggregate net profit was Rs. 12.03 crores. Owing to improved and efficient operations, the Gujarat Electricity Board, which had incurred a loss of Rs. 543.35 crores during 1982-83, turned the corner and made a profit of Rs. 1383.77 crores during the year 1983-84. The break-up details of 23 profit-making units and 12 loss-making units are given in Table-5.4(a) and Table-5.4(b) respectively.

TABLE-5.4(B)

Sl. No	*Name of the Enterprise*	*Profit during 1983-84 (Rs. in Lakhs)*	*Result of 1982-83 Profit (+) Loss (-) (Rs. in Lakhs)*
1	2	3	4
1.	Gujarat Rural Industries Marketing Corporation Ltd.	11.33	(-) 6.25
2.	Gujarat State Forest Development Corporation Ltd.	21.86	(-) 9.97
3.	Gujarat State Handicrafts & Handloom	14.43	(-) 15.49
4.	Gujarat State Land Development Corporation Ltd.	26.21	(-) 19.94
5.	Gujarat Tractor Corporation Ltd.	244.27	(-) 231.30
6.	Gujarat Water Resources Development Corporation	65.90	(-) 77.72
7.	Tourism Corporation of Gujarat Ltd.	26.49	(+) 2.41
8.	Girnar Scooters Ltd.	32.14	--
9.	Polymers Corporation of Gujarat Ltd.	249.44	(-) 330.58
10.	Gujarat Housing Board	107.29	(+) 35.56
11.	Gujarat Slum Clearance Board	7.54	(+) 6.89
12.	Gujarat State Road Transport Corporation	527.95	(-) 554.91
	Total	1334.85	(-) 1201.30

Out of the 50 enterprises the following enterprises had not commenced production, but had completed one year commencement of activities upto 31st March, 1984. Besides the above, the Gujarat Electricity Board and the Gujarat State Road Transport Corporation occupy an important position among the Public Enterprises in the State, which could be viewed from the following Table-5.6. It is evident that the results of these two enterprises would affect the overall results of the Public Enterprises in the State. The total loss of Public Enterprises is of the order of Rs. 20.36 crores in 1982-83. The Gujarat State Electricity Board and the Gujarat State Road Transport Corporation accounted losses of Rs. 5.43 crores and Rs. 5.55 crores, respectively. The following Table (Table 5.7) indicates the position regarding the internal resources generated by the Public Enterprises system during the year 1983-84.

TABLE 5.5

1.	Gujarat State Petro-Chemicals Corporation Ltd.
2.	Gujarat Insecticides Ltd.
3.	Gujarat Amino Chemicals Ltd.
4.	Cement Corporation of Gujarat Ltd.
5.	Gujarat Hotels Baroda Ltd.
6.	Gujarat Mulco Electronics Ltd.
7.	Gujarat Nylons Ltd.
8.	Gujarat Trans-Receivers Ltd.
9.	Gujarat Tyres Ltd.
10.	Steel Corporation of Gujarat Ltd.
11.	*Gujarat State Civil Supplies Corporation Ltd.
12.	*Gujarat Scheduled Castes Economic Development Corporation Ltd.
13.	*Gujarat Water Supply and Sewerage Board

* The accounts for 1983-84 are not available.

TABLE 5.6

Investment Patterns in SLPEs in Gujarat

Sl.Item	*Gujarat Electricity Board*	*Gujarat State Road Transport Corporation*	*Other Enterprises*	*Total*
1. Financial Resources (%) (31.3.84)	58.82	4.11	37.07	100
2. Investment of State Government (%)	68.89	7.52	23.59	100
3. Capital employed (%) 31.3.84	57.49	2.83	39.68	100
4. Turnover (%)	49.89	22.20	27.91	100
5. Profit(+) Loss (-) Rs. in crores (1983-84)	13.84	(-)5.28	3.47	12.03

TABLE 5.7

Year	*Profit after tax but before investment allowance reserve*	*Depreciation*	*Total internal Resources (2+3)*
1979-80	(-)14.20	35.53	21.33
1980-81	(-) 67.70	42.50	(-) 25.20
1981-82	(-) 39.82	47.45	7.63
1982-83	(-) 9.05	53.76	44.71
1983-84	12.03	61.53	73.56

Perhaps the performance of the Public Enterprises during 1983-84 has been considerably improved when compared with its last four year's performance due to improved operations.

Status of SLPEs in Gujarat

The financial profile of SLPEs in Gujarat are given in Table 5.8.

TABLE 5.8

Status of SLPEs in Gujarat

Years / *Items*	*1998-99*	*1999-00*	*2000-01*	*2001-02*	*2002-03*	*2003-04*
1. Total no.of SLPEs	38	46	50	50	50	50
2. No.of Working SLPEs	33	39	40	40	40	40
3. No.of Non-Working SLPEs	5	7	10	10	10	
(i) Under Liquidation	4	4	4		4	
(ii) Under Closure			3		6	
(iii) Under Merger	.					
(iv) Others	1	3	3			
4. Total Equity	6052.29	7714.96	9390.36	10429.01	10629.28	13113.27
5. Total Debt	3534.28	11507.74	14047.36	15142.63	15028.86	21436.93
6. Total Investment	9586.57	19222.70	23437.72	25571.64	25758.14	34550.20
7. No.of Profit making enterprises	–	20	20	22	22	22
8. No.of Loss making enterprises	–	22	22	25	24	24
9. Net Profit/Loss	–	-147.24	-736.65	-2722.20	-3107.39	-754.92
10. Accumulated Loss(-)/Profit	4752.36	-874.17	-964.78	-3663.82	-6774.48	-7206.74

Source: Reports of the Comptroller and Auditor General of India (Commercial), on Gujarat for 1998-99 to 2003-04.

Management

The management consists of Board of Directors, part-time Chairman, who is usually official, a full-time Managing Director or Chief Executive Officer, normally appointed on deputation from the Government amongst the Civil Servants and part-time Directors, both official and non-official. There are also variations 'of this pattern like full-time Chairman-cum-Managing Director and full-time Chairman and full-time Managing Director which could be viewed from the data given in Table-5.8.

The management below the Board level, consisting of several posts like General Managers, Deputy General Managers and Managers, etc., is created by the respective Boards barring a few exceptions where statutory rules of appointments are required to be made by the Government or with the approval of the Government. Normally, the following sources are contacted for deployment of Chief Executive in Public Enterprises, and the table indicates the different categories of Civil Servants deployed in various undertakings. (Table-5.8).

TABLE 5. 9

Sl.No	*Pattern*	*No. of. Enterprises*
1	Full-time chairman and a few full-time members	1
2	Full-time chairman and a few full-time Managing Director	5
3	Full-time Chairman-cum-Managing Director	1
4	Part-time Chairman and Full-time Managing Director or Chief Executive	43
	Total	50

Social Obligations

The public sector enterprises system in the State of Gujarat has generated a direct employment to 1,18,590 persons as on 31st March, 1984, as compared to 1,06,259 persons employed as on 31st March, 1982 and 1,13,320 persons employed as on March, 1983, registering a phenomenal growth in the employment generation pattern, besides facilitating lot of employment by way of in- direct assistance. The two Public Enterprises viz., Gujarat Electricity Board and Gujarat State Transport Corporation accounted for 35,211 and 49,233 employees, respectively. During the period as on 31st March 1982, 1983 and 1984, the capital employed per employee ratio works out to Rs. 1.21 lakhs, 1.28. lakhs and 1.42 lakhs for all the enterprises put together, respectively." Besides these, the Public Sector Enterprises have also contributed several crores of rupees to the exchequer by way of direct and indirect taxes and also provided lot of employment opportunities to ST, SC and BC persons. Perhaps, there may be an imperative necessity to take account about the onerous social obligations these Pubic Sector Enterprises are discharging while evaluating their performance in terms of return on investment made into the system

Problems

The problems of the Public Sector Enterprises in the State are varied in nature. There are a variety of problems faced by the Public Sector Enterprises. Amidst several important problems the prominent one appears to be the delay in finalising the annual accounts. There are a number of Public Enterprises which did not finalise their annual accounts for a variety of reasons. The list of enterprises which have not finalised the accounts in time are given in Table 5.9.

TABLE 5.10

Sl. No	*Name of Enterprises*	*Last date of the accounting year for which audited accounts are not available*
1.	Gujarat Agro Industries Corporation Ltd.	31.3.81
2.	Gujarat Rural Industries Marketing Corporation Ltd.	31.3.81
		31.3.82
		31.3.83
		31.3.84
3.	Gujarat Sheep and Wool Development Corporation Ltd.	31.3.83
		31.3.84
4.	Gujarat State Civil Supplies Corporation Ltd.	30.9.81
		30.9.82
		30.9.83
5.	Gujarat State Construction Corporation Ltd.	31.7.81
		31.7.82
		31.7.83

6.	Gujarat State Handicrafts and Handloom Development Corporation Ltd.	31.3.82
		31.3.83
		31.3.84
7.	Gujarat State Handloom Development Corporation Ltd.	31.3.82
		31.3.83
		31.3.84
8.	Gujarat State Land Development Corporation Ltd.	30.6.80
		30.6.81
		30.6.82
		30.6.83
9.	Gujarat Tractor Corporation Ltd.	31.3.82
		31.3.83
		31.3.84
10.	Gujarat Water Resources Development Corporation Ltd.	31.7.79
		31.7.80
		31.7.81
		31.7.82
		31.7.83
		31.7.84
11.	Tourism Corporation of Gujarat Ltd.	31.3.84
12.	Gujarat Insecticides Ltd.	30.6.82
		30.9.83
13.	Steel Corporation of Gujarat Ltd.	31.3.84
14.	Gujarat Housing Board	31.3.84
15.	Gujarat Rural Housing Board	31.3.84
16.	Gujarat Municipal Finance Board	31.3.83
17.	Gujarat State Road Transport Corporation	31.3.84
18.	Gujarat slum Clearance	31.3.84
19.	Gujarat Water Supply & Sewerage Board	31.3.84
20.	Gujarat Scheduled Caste Economic Development Corporation Ltd.	1982-83
21.	Gujarat State Civil Supplies Corporation Ltd.	1982-83
22.	Gujarat Water Supply & Sewerage Board	1982-83

A similar study of delay in the finalisation of annual accounts was undertaken by the Institute of Public Enterprise. The research findings showed that a variety of reasons are responsible for this problem. Prominent among them were the delay in the appointment of auditors by the Government on the recommendations of the Comptroller & Auditor General and lack of interest on the part of the management to get the accounts finalised quickly, lack of professional staff, induction of departmental personnel in the company who do not have the requisite professional competence with the result of delaying the accounts for want of knowledge in double entry book-keeping system, periodical change of chief executives without fixation of minimum tenure etc. Perhaps this is an important area where the Government may try to remedy the situation with suitable measures.

Conclusion

Undoubtedly, there is a phenomenal growth in the Public Enterprises system and the Public Enterprises proliferation into different walks of life of the civilian life in the Government of Gujarat. The huge amount of resources pumped, the performance achieved by the Public Enterprises in terms of financial parameters which could be viewed from Table-10, is an indication that there is a substantial improvement in the operation of the Public Sector Enterprises with regard to achievement of objective goals as well as financial results. Still, there appears to be ample scope for the improvement of these Public Sector Enterprises. Perhaps, the measures to be taken for the improvement of performance may vary from one Public Sector Enterprise to another Public Sector Enterprise. However, certain general measures like professionalisation of the Boards, management, observation of scientific principles of management, strict vigil over the Public Enterprise performance performance by nodal agencies like the Bureau of Public Enterprises will pave the way for the desired goal of Public Enterprise system, viz., reaching the commanding heights of efficient economy.

Suggestions

1. The Public Enterprises should develop corporate plans clearly demarcating the short-term plans, long-term plans capable of coping with environmental changes (strategic changes) possessing built-in flexibility.
2. The planned results may be monitored on a half-yearly basis under the guidance of a Committee consisting of the Secretary under whose administrative control the enterprise runs, the Chief Executive of the enterprise, the Director-General, PEMB, and officials of the Planning and Finance Department.
3. There is need to professionalise the management, develop a senior managerial cadre of well-trained professionally competent and committed executives, willing to undertake challenging assignments. Besides professional staff. Government may even draft services of some of the competent and promising bureaucrats to man key positions provided they are fully confident of achieving the desired objective goals of the enterprise.
4. Government should have a machinery like the Public Enterprise Management Board to constantly keep vigil over the performance of the industries and suitably recommend for a system of rewards, punishments and redressals.
5. A system should be evolved whereby the pioneer training institutions like the Institute of Public Enterprise, Public Enterprises Management Board, Administrative Staff College of India may endeavour to train the personnel right from the level of Chief Executive down to the lowest staff in their respective

fields mainly to keep themselves abreast of the latest developments in different areas of management.

6. The criteria for investments in various parts of the State should be based on technical feasibilities and financial viabilities, having due regard to employment potentiality.
7. The financial controls are to be administered right from the commencement of the new project and it should be ensured that the project cost escalations are kept under absolute control with the help of PERT/CPM techniques.
8. The Public Enterprises should administer sound financial management with particular relevance to financing and investment decisions. Wherever possible, some of the big enterprises may prefer to have promising professional accountants as Finance Directors to guide the Boards in those areas.
9. The Government may endeavour to start a commercial bank growth fund with which it can cater to the ways and means of positions of different Public Enterprises so as to maintain cost of funds more economically.
10. The enterprises may be advised to step in capital market to mobilise funds in the form of debentures, shares, etc. The institutional finances from the Apex financial institutions like the IDBI. IFCI. IRCI (even World Bank), may be availed, taking advantage of concessional rate of finance.
11. The Government may have a small Cell responsible for keeping track of the dividend/interest monies receivable from enterprises from time to time.
12. Depending upon the peculiarities of the enterprise, there may be a 2-tier or 3-tier management information system which can assist effectively in the decision making process.

TABLE 5.11

Public Enterprises in Gujarat at a Glance

1	2	*31-3-78* 3	*31-3-79* 4	*31-3-80* 5	*31-3-81* 6	*31-3-82* 7	*31-3-83* 8	*31-3-84* 9
1.	Total No. of Public Enterprises	35	39	43	46	48	50	50
2.	No. of enterprises having completed one year of production/business activities	29	32	35	36	37	38	40
3.	No. of enterprises whose accounts have been taken into consideration for the purpose of the statement	28	31	34	35	34	34	36
4.	Total financial resources (Rs. in crores)	1014.54	1195.50	1443.18	1758.73	2153.14	2726.27	3008.31
5.	Total investment by State Government (Rs. in crores)	415.72	493.60	606.85	756.30	865.76	1190.00	1404.72
6.	Capital employed (Rs. in crores)	762	738	1113	1445	1287	1456	1685
7.	No. of employees (in thousands)	N.A	79	91	97	106	113	119
		1977-78	1978-79	1979-80	1980-81	1981-82	1982-83	1983-84

13. Government may prefer to advise the Public Enterprises concerned to fill up the top posts like Finance Director, General Manager (Finance) from within the result-oriented finance professionals like Chartered Accountants and Cost Accountants, dispense with the system of deputation from Accountant-General's Department and fix the responsibility on the Finance Director for the timely finalisation of annual accounts.
14. The Public Enterprises especially in the sector of production of consumer goods and engineering products, may adopt suitable aggressive marketing techniques/strategies for boosting their sales wherever possible.
15. Depending upon the suitability of the enterprises, it may be endeavoured to set up a Management Services Department' in the undertakings with the complement of professionals like a qualified Cost Accountant, Industrial Engineer, O & M experts, etc., to advise the management on enhancement of productivity with the help of techniques like cost reduction, cost control, etc.

REFERENCES

Public Enterprises VII *Annual Report, 1983-84,* Bureau of Public Enterprises, Government of Gujarat, Bombay.

Delay in the Finalisation of Annual Accounts--A Research Study conducted by Shri S.S.T. Sai, Research Officer, Institute of Public Enterprise, Hyderabad.

The Research Study on the Return on Public Investment in the Government of Andhra Pradesh, conducted by the Institute of Public Enterprise, Hyderabad.

6

Development and Performance of State Level Public Enterprises of Karnataka

*T.P. Issar**

This paper traces the public enterprise tradition in Karnataka, presents their profile and discusses in detail the working of Karnataka State Electricity Board and the Karnataka Road Transport Corporation -the two major SLPEs in the State. The paper expresses its concern for a low profitability of the SLPEs and suggests the toning up of the institution of Managing Directors, long tenure for the Chief Executives and extensive MIS system to do away with this malaise.

Karnataka's tradition of what is now known as the public sector goes back to the late twenties and the early thirties. Its long history in this area of State Enterprises is explained by the fact that the State was lucky to have administrator-visionaries like Sir M. Visveswaraya. These ventures, which were governmental undertakings in the earlier stages, were conceived of and set up primarily with a view to exploiting the available resources of raw material and power in certain localities, creating pockets of industrialisation, with the

* Director-General, Karnataka State Bureau of Public Enterprises, Department of Personnel and Administrative Reforms, Government of Karnataka, Bangalore.

resultant employment opportunities and a variety of economic spin-offs.

Much time has elapsed since then and the economic scenario has undergone momentous changes. In many cases, the circumstances and considerations which provided the initial justification for setting up these ventures have either changed beyond recognition or do not exist at all. To cite an example, Visveswaraya Iron and Steel Ltd. (formerly Mysore Iron and Steel Ltd., Bhadravathi) was set up with a view to exploit the locally available iron-ore, with easy availability of plentiful hydro- electric power. Its raison d'etre, after decades of economic changes and developments, is no longer the local economy, and the pricing and marketing of its products are dictated almost entirely by national and international market-compulsions. It has developed into a big-time manufacturing company in a line in which it is now having to compete with much bigger rivals in the national market, and having to countenance and overcome almost insuperable problems like the rapidly escalating cost of power and massive power cuts leading to a very low-level utilisation of installed capacity.

A phenomenon which has made its appearance somewhat recently in this sector is the undertakings set up in the State (as in other States) in the purely developmental and public services fields of activity like public transport and welfare of backward classes. The criterion for judging the performance of the undertakings in these categories is, in the nature of things, somewhat different from the angles from which industrial undertakings are judged. The profit criterion has necessarily to take the secondary place in the case of these undertakings, although it is being increasingly recognised that even among these undertakings, the assigned socio-economic objectives are carried out best by the ones which can manage to operate profitably.

Then there are the marketing or trading enterprises, some of which partake of the character of service enterprises in certain respects while doing, by and large, agencyship, trading or marketing. Their performance, again, is judged principally by the criterion of profitability, besides fulfilment of the assigned objectives.

There are also statutory bodies like the Karnataka Electricity Board and the KSRTC. Many of their operations are kept deliberately unremunerative as a matter of State policy with a view to benefit specific sections of the population. These are in the nature of services and utilities which are, again, not judged, in the nature of things, from the criterion purely of profitability.

The authorised and paid-up share capital of State Public Sector Undertakings in Karnataka ranges from Rs. 10 lakhs to Rs. 4 lakhs to Rs. 75 crores and Rs. 74.22 crores respectively. Government's share-holding in these ranges from 51% to 100%. Government's total share-holding in these undertakings is of the order of Rs. 323.43 crores. Besides, Government has advanced loans to them totalling Rs. 1031.14 crores.

On an analysis of the growth of the Public Sector in Karnataka State during the last 3 decades. It is seen that as many as 30 Public Sector Enterprises were set up in State during the decade 1970-80. Against the up-to-date number of 53 Enterprises, there were only 10 in 1950. 19 in 1965 and 29 in 1970. The nuluber went up to 46 in 1975. The up-to-date number mentioned above, does not include some enterprises which have been wound up or merged with others. Those which are in the process of merger have also not been taken into account. The increase has been the largest in the manufacturing enterprises followed by developmental enterprises. As stated above, the total share capital investment in the Public Sector Enterprises by the Government of

Karnataka, as 00 31-3-86, amounted to Rs. 330.00 crores. The total resources at the disposal of the Public Sector Enterprises of Karnataka as on 31-3-85 amounted to Rs. 3629.24 crores while their reserves and surplus amounted to Rs. 368.63 crore& on the said date. Of the loans borrowed by the Public Sector Enterprises, amounting to Rs. 1993.06 as on 31-3-85, the State Government's lending amounted to Rs. 1031.14 crores, the rest coming largely from the financial industries. The, total investment in terms of share capital and loans amounted to Rs. 2450.06 as on 31-3-85. The gross income of the Public Sector Enterprises of Karnataka as on 31-3-85 was Rs. 1356.72 crores. On the whole, there was a net loss of Rs. 31.22 crores during 1985-86 as against a loss of Rs. 40.56 crores during the previous year.

There is a tendency to judge the performance of the public sector enterprises as a whole in terms of the net loss or profit in a year. It is indeed important that the public sector enterprises should be able to plough back generated income, after retaining a reasonable share of profits and providing for development or expansion plans, if any. However, as indicated above, the criterion of profitability has necessarily to take second place while judging the performance of enterprises like the KEB and the KSRTC. These enterprises are in the nature of services and utilities and the losses incurred by them can significantly change the overall performance of the public sector. It may be pointed out here that the overall loss of Rs. 31.22 crores recorded by the public sector enterprises of Karnataka during 1985-86 includes the loss of Rs. 17.02 crores incurred by the State Electricity Board and Rs. 12 crores by the State Road Transport Corporation.

As regards (Karnataka Electricity Board) KEB, it is to be appreciated that it had to purchase power from the neighbouring States at a huge cost during a drought year. Again, it has to subsidise operations, as a matter of State policy, in the rural/agricultural sector. Any move on its part to raise the power tariff meets with stiff resistance and it is only very recently that the Board revised the tariff.

As for the State Road Transport Corporation, its loss though it declined appreciably compared to the previous 3 years is explained by the higher working cost and the unremunerative fare-structuring. Transport services have to be run in many unremunerative areas, again as a matter of State policy, because even in areas of the State where public transport has not yet been nationalised it is seen that private operators ignore such sectors leaving it to the State Transport Undertaking to step in. Yet even in the case of this undertaking there is always stiff resistance to any attempt at revision of the fare structure.

What I am driving at is that there are certain areas of public service or consumer needs where the public sector has necessarily to have a strong or exclusive presence because the presence of the private sector in those areas is either negligent or weak. Again, public utilities and services provided by the State through public sector undertakings serve the ideal of a socialistic order in which these services and utilities of mass use or consumption are provided at deliberately controlled prices even at conscious loss" to the exchequer. Therefore, the balance sheet of such undertakings should not be given the same kind of scrutiny as is done in the case of production enterprises. The same consideration would also apply to undertakings which have been set up by the State with a view to benefiting target groups like small entrepreneurs looking for industrial projects which offer promise, leather artisans, craftsmen engaged in producing handicrafts, and entrepreneurs from weaker sections who have to be helped with seed-money for raising loans for their professional needs. Enterprises in these lines in Karnataka include enterprises, many of them set up during the last decade, like the Handloom

Development Corporation, Leather Industries Development Corporation, Electronics Development Corporation, Handicrafts Development Corporation, Scheduled Castes and Scheduled Tribes Development Corporation, Backward Classes and Minorities Development Corporation, etc. As many as 30 Public Sector Enterprises (of the present enterprises) were set up in the State during the decade 1970-80. The increase has been the largest in the manufacturing enterprises followed by developmental enterprises.

Even as regards the production group of public sector enterprises the turnover, size of investment and the scale of operations varies quite widely. Thus if a fairly large number of small enterprises makė a profit, it can be totally obscured by the loss incurred by just one or two enterprises. For instance, the losses of Visveswaraya Iron and Steel Ltd. have mounted from just under a crore in 1981-82 to 31.79 crores in 1985-86. In spite of the said loss incurred by just one enterprise during the year, the overall loss incurred by the public sector enterprises, after taking into account the total profits earned by the profit- making enterprises, was Rs. 31.22 crores. In other words, the overall loss would not have been there but for the loss incurred by just one company are prone to block out of view some were visible improvements recorded by many enterprises.

A recent study of the apportionment of and return or investment in the State Public Sector Enterprises reveals that 01 the total investment of Rs. 1730.80 crores in the 58 enterprises, about 80% to mounting to Rs. 1382 crorest is invested in the 21 enterprises which made a profit during the year 1985-86. The return on the total equity share capital invested in the above mentioned profit-making enterprises amounted to 24.45% while the return on the total investment (share capital plus loans amounting to Rs. 1730.80 crores as stated above) amounted to 2.53%. If the loans advanced by the State

Government and the lending institutions of the State alone are taken into account the return 01 su£h loans by the said profit-making enterprises amounted to 4.98%.

Looking at the entire picture of return on investment whether in the profit-making enterprises or the losing ones the percentage works out to 0.96. If however, the equity contribution and lending by the State Government alone are taken into account, the return on total investment works out to 1.93%. To sum up, the picture emerging from the point of view of return on investment, as on 31-3-1986, is a very satisfactory one if the return on profit-making enterprises alone is taken into account However, the return on the total investment in all the enter- prises is hardly one percent; it will improve slightly the total investment by the State Government alone is taken into account.

Government of Karnataka is constantly reviewing the role o the public sector from various points of view the most important being the need of the State's presence in any sector o public service or consumer need, besides other important parameters of changes in the economy during the recent decades advances in technology leading to displacement of labour i certain lines of production and the new realities of pricing and marketing which operate at a national level rather than a regional or local level. It has been increasingly realised that there is nothing sacrosanct about the original objectives behind setting up many of the State's Public Sector Enterprises. It has been recognised that a Public Sector Undertaking, regardless of whether in the industrial line or in the development or service line, will have to be ultimately judged by its ability, after long and reasonable enough gestation period, to generate its own resources for growth. If it becomes a continuing and increasing burden on the exchequer, there cannot be a more positive indication of its failure to carry out the socio-economic objectives assigned to it. There is a limit to the doses of equity and loan assistance which the State can spare even for developmental, services enterprises and public utilities.

Karnataka is passing through a phase of serious constraints on its financial resources resulting from four successive drought years. It is therefore, having to husband its resources with extreme care. With this background it is being impressed on the State Public Sector Enterprises that they must put in the necessary effort towards raising institutional finance, both as regards the funds required for capital investment as well as the working capital. Such an approach to funding the Public Sector Enterprises was in any case warranted because they often tend to opt for the easier method of seeking equity or loan assistance from the State Government without putting in any serious efforts towards procuring the required funds from other sources, expecting the State Government to help out only with the interest liability. One great advantage of these enterprises approaching financial institutions rather than the State Government would be that the required thinking and planning would go into making their schemes bankable especially as regards production enterprises. In any case, their schemes must pass through the test of bankability regardless of whether the funds ultimately come from the State Government or the financial institutions.

Another important area which is attracting serious attention from the State Government is the lack of proper and prompt feed-back from Government nominee directors on the boards of directors of Public Sector Undertakings. There have been many instances where nominee directors failed not only to attend important board meetings but even to keep themselves apprised of the proceedings of meetings. In some cases, patently objectionable resolutions were based, involving sizeable expenditure and outlays, without the State Government being aware of what was happening. Whereas the State Government does not want to unduly interfere with the autonomy of the Public Sector Enterprises, it understandably wants its nominee directors to properly and adequately represent the State's views, leaving it to the board of directors to take an appropriate decision on the overall merits of a resolution.

Carefully formulated guidelines have been issued in this to all nominee directors and these are reiterated from time.

The State Government is also becoming increasingly aware of the importance of stability of tenure of chief executives of public sector enterprises. It is being increasingly realised that not only should the selection to the post of chief executive of a public sector undertaking be based on proven flair and integrity but once an appointment has been made the executive should be allowed a reasonable spell of time at least 3 to 4 years if not more.

Lastly, a word about the role which the State Bureau of Public Enterprises is playing in policy-formulation at the State Level regarding the functioning of public sector enterprises as also in providing regular feed-back to the State on the performance of these enterprises, judged from important criteria and parameters of profitability and purposeful operation both as regards production enterprises, which constitute about 40% of the total number of the state public sector enterprises, but represent as much as 72 percent of the State's investment in the public sector, and the other categories of public sector enter- prises like utilities, service enterprises and developmental enterprises.

As a nodal agency which was set up in 1980 at the instance of the Government of India, the Karnataka State Bureau of Enterprises has set up an Information System for monitoring performance of the Public Sector Undertakings and sending to State Government periodical reports, drawing special attention trends which need to be taken careful note of. The Bureau set up expert panels which are manned by people drawn from State Public Sector Enterprises themselves, representing lines of specialisation and management expertise. These are given specific issues, problems and scenarios for study comment. The result of these exercises supplements and depth to the studies done by the Bureau's own staff. The Bureau thus, keeps the State Government up-to-date with warning signals which call for immediate attention and remedial or reconstructive measures. The Bureau has a say in all matters of fresh investment of funds in the State Public

TABLE 6.1

Status of SLPEs in Karnataka

Items	*Years* 2000-01	2001-02	2002-03	2003-04
1. Total no.of SLPEs	76	76	80	82
2. No.of Working SLPEs	63	63	64	65
3. No.of Non-Working SLPEs	13	13	16	17
(i) Under liquidation				
(ii) Under Closure	12	12		
(iii) Under Merger	1	1		
(iv) Others				
4. Total Equity	6116.81	7697.33	10,137.65	12,591.72
5. Total Debt	13099.96	14981.7	16,407.48	21,105.38
6. Total Investment	19216.77	22679.03	26,545.13	33,697.10
7. No.of Profit making enterprises	26	32	34	34
8. No.of Loss making enterprises	36	38	16	16
9. Net Profit/Loss	-318.22	104.23	--	143.41
10. Accumulated Loss(-)/Profit	-225.24	-228.03	--	-843.75

Source: Reports of the Comptroller and Auditor General of India (Commercial), on Karnataka for 2000-01 to 2003-04.

Sector Enterprises prescribed limit, as also in questions of disinvestment enterprises which have lost their raison d'etre in the public sector.

Status of SLPEs in Karnataka

The Table 6.1 presents the status of SLPEs as on March 31st 2004.

7

Performance and Development of State Level Enterprises in Kerala

*R. Narayanan**

Kerala is one State where the number of public enterprises has gone up phenomenally. *The paper outlines the classification of SLPEs in the State to pinpoint the difference between the approach followed in Kerala vis-a-vis the other states. The paper laments about the low profitability of the SLPEs and singles out labour unrest and management failure as the principal causes for this phenomenon. The paper suggests, an aggressive marketing strategy, promotion of PE oriented corporate culture, reduction in overmanning and improving the project management as the elements of an integrated strategy to turn the corner for the SLPEs in the spate.*

Kerala State perhaps stands in the forefront regarding the number of public sector undertakings in a single State. As on 31.3.1986 there were 96 state level undertakings, which include 88 government companies and 8 statutory bodies. Out of the 88 companies, 24 are subsidiaries. The growth in the number of public sector undertakings was maximum during the 70's. Therefore, they have not increased very much and currently there is a distinct sign of the growth being arrested because of economic considerations and a greater

* Commissioner and Secretary, Department of Finance, Government of Kerala.

awareness among the political executive that proliferation of enterprises could result in unmanageable liabilities.

The 88 Government companies together had State Government investment amounting to Rs. 214.84 crores and the 8 statutory bodies had an investment amounting to Rs. 61.06 crores. The Government companies and statutory bodies have traditionally been considered as sources of conferring employment opportunities. Available statistics indicate that the Government companies had on their rolls 73,907 employees including 31,285 seasonal workers. The statutory bodies had 66,963 employees. The seasonal workers are mainly employed by the Kerala State Cashew Development Corporation where the work is highly seasonal.

The undertakings could be broadly classified into 15 groups. They are:

1. Development & Infrastructural agencies
2. Electronics
3. Engineering
4. Chemicals
5. Textiles
6. Electricals
7. Ceramics and Refractories
8. Plantation and agro-based industries
9. Wood-based industries
10. Traditional industries
11. Trading units
12. Public Utilities
13. Welfare agencies
14. Others; and
15. Statutory bodies

A group-wise study has not been undertaken although the relevant data is available in the publications brought out by the Bureau of Public Enterprises of the Government. The working results indicate that the statutory bodies have, by and large, earned profits whereas the Government companies as a whole have lost heavily. The reason for Government companies sustaining heavy losses is not hard to analyse. They are numerous but could be broadly classified as lack of corporate culture, low profitability, poor marketing approaches, financial difficulties in the form of heavy interest payments on debts, and, by and large, lack of professionalism in management. The Economic Review which is brought out by the Government as part of the annual budget documents has indicated that the accumulated losses of the Government companies as at the end of 1985-86 stood at Rs. 125.88 crores. The details of the public sector industrial undertakings whose accumulated losses exceeded their paid up capital is given in the Annexure.

Some peculiar features in relation to the public enterprises functioning in Kerala might be worth discussing in the context of trying to improve the overall performance.

The production losses as a result of labour unrest and other reasons like power-cut and breakdown of machinery are fairly high in Kerala. It is well-known that multiplicity of trade unions causes losses in man-days with each one vying with the other for establishing a stranglehold on labour. There are instances of wild cat strikes being called even when disciplinary action is taken by the management on chronic cases of indiscipline. Apart from the militancy of the unions, Kerala, by and large, represents a State where wages are high and production is low. This is a serious situation for which no ready answer can be found. The dominating role of the unions and their nexus with the political executive results in frequent government intervention in pushing up wages even in loss-making units. Wage revisions and bonus payments are considered as inevitable. A disturbing feature of the scenario is that most of the public enterprises in Kerala are today functioning almost as appendages of the State Government. The management very often consists of chosen representatives of the ruling party and in some cases even the middle and lower level managers are appointees of the government. Easy access of such persons to the ministers causes friction between the chief executives and the ministers. It is necessary to ensure complete autonomy in the functioning of the internal management of public sector enterprises. In this context, as an extension to this phenomenon, one also notices that the boards of directors are parked with people having political contacts. The result is that the boards of directors are not very effective. Official representation in the board also leaves much to be desired. Putting it simply it can well be said that the dismal performance of the Government companies *is* primarily on account of lack of professionalism at various levels in the managerial sector.

While the management aspect is well established as a factor contributing to the lack of progress, another specific reason is the fact that many of the undertakings have tried to launch ambitious projects that have long gestation periods, which as a result cause time and cost over-runs. The project reports look promising on paper. However, on implementation, several snags develop and the Government is forced to sanction upward revision of the final cost of the project from time to time. Most of such projects are financed not only from Government equity participation but almost always through loans from institutional agencies like the IDBI, IFCI or a consortium of banks. The upward revision of projects no doubt has to be cleared in inter- institutional group meetings, but very often institutions insist upon not only an enhancement of government's contribution but also on government guarantees sometimes without even allowing the usual guarantee commission. Such conditions impose a heavy strain on the plan budgets of the state which can hardly accommodate the over-runs. There is no escape of the situation because of the fact that considerable progress is usually already achieved and there is no point in leaving the project in midstream. In this context, I would also like to mention the current situation Where in serious attempts are being made to rehabilitate many of the undertakings that are in difficulties but which have a potential for development. These companies are not necessarily sick but they are on the verge of being so. Therefore, the government are interested in salvaging them to the best of their ability. Here again, the same kind of package proposals are initiated involving considerable additional government finance both direct and indirect. While the direct financing consists of making available share capital or direct loans on soft terms, the indirect method consists of converting the existing loans into equity and in several cases by deferment of sales-tax payable over a period of years. This is to make the end product competitive but it causes serious drop in the revenue resources of the State.

Employment generation being the prime objective of the state government, there is extreme reluctance on the part of the government to layoff or retrench workers. Even in well-established undertakings, they are over-staffed both at the managerial and the workers 'level.' The overhead costs are some times beyond the reach of the undertaking and when the question of payment of bonus is considered, the government are forced to step in by the grant of ad hoc special allowance to some of the undertakings like the RTC. In the RTC there is also a pension scheme for the workers, which apart from being a perennial drain on the resources of the Corporation, causes imbalances in the budget of the Corporation, because of periodical upward revision in pension and the persistent demand for extending liberal changes in family pensions of the central and state governments.

A sluggish marketing strategy is also a factor to be considered as a serious issue when one considers the overall performance of the enterprises. However, this is balanced by the availability of a ready market on many of the goods produced by State level enterprises. In fact some of the undertakings enjoy a monopoly in the Indian market e.g., Travancore Titanium Products and the Kerala Minerals and Metals Limited, both of which use the beach sand which consists of chemicals like blumnate rutile and zircon for producing Tatanium-di-oxide which enjoys a captive market. There are undertakings which have a shelf of good orders; an example of which is TELK, set up with Japanese collaboration and having orders from several state electricity boards. The Agro-based undertakings of the State have a promising future, particularly the Oil Palm India Limited, which is expected to produce palm oil within the state. This has a good market throughout the country. The electronic units of the State which are facing fierce competition today have earned a good name in the domestic market with KELTRON leading the field. There is ample scope for further development of the traditional industries where the talent is abundant and the work force available is plenty. The need of the country's production in the traditional sector has already been recognised and one of the main strategies in the ensuing years of the plan will be to adopt modern technology in the traditional sector without hampering the employment potential.

As far as the state governments are concerned the dividends accruing to it from the enterprises cannot be considered as a major revenue item. As a matter of fact, only 8 enterprises paid any dividend to the Government and the total amount paid is less than Rs. 2 crores. However, the real interest of the government is in sustaining these enterprises and ensuring that their dependence on government for finances is minimised in the quickest possible time.

A nodal agency to oversee the general working of the enterprises is the State Bureau of Public Enterprises. Till recently the Chief Secretary of the State was himself the Chairman of the Bureau certain Senior Secretaries to Government its members and three professional managers. All expansion and diversification projects of existing undertakings as well as the setting up of new units have to be cleared by the BPE and in several cases remedial measures are suggested like engagement of consultants amalgamation of enterprises and specific measures to generate enthusiasm and response to the units. A final word may be mentioned about the need to ensure continuity in the tenures of the executives chosen for leading an organisation. Unfortunately there is a dearth of personnel and the result is that the All India Service officers are posted in a routine way in the undertakings. Some of them do not have the needed commitment and are unable to build up a corporate culture. Even if they had the ability, initiated and the willingness, their tenures are shortened because of other compulsions which push them out to different fields. It is perhaps necessary to gradually evolve a cadre of personnel within the state who will be exclusively earmarked to undertakings without being changed every now and then. Existing results have shown that where the tenure of the chief executive has been long enough, the results have been better.

TABLE 7.1

Financial Position of SLPEs in Kerala

(Rs. in lakhs)

S. No.	Name of Company	Paid-up Accumulated capital losses	(as on 31.3.1986)
(1)	(2)	(3)	(4)
	Keltron Group		
1.	Keltron Counters Ltd.	223.30	331.38
2.	Keltron Electro Ceramics Ltd.	89.59	172.36
3.	Keltron Resisors Ltd.	67.56	105.71
4.	Keltron Power Devices Ltd.	175.30	426.16
5.	Keltron Rectifiers Ltd.	157.26	304.22
	Kerala State Industrial Enterprises Group		
6.	The Kerala Ceramics Ltd.	205.33	828.16
7.	Kerala Soaps and Oils Ltd.	185.59	752.38
8.	Tranvancore Plywood Industries Ltd.	48.59	166.44
9.	Kerala State Detergents and Chemicals Ltd.	154.63	356.10
	Chemicals		
10.	The Kerala Minerals and Metals Ltd.	2756.27	2842.06
	Textiles		
11.	Trivandrum Spinning Mills Ltd.	184.99	303.19
12.	Sitaram Textiles Ltd.	267.00	829.46
	Electricals and Cables		
13.	The Metropolitan Engg. Co. Ltd.	33.17	180.74
14.	United Electrical Industries Ltd.	136.40	205.58
15.	Transformers & Electricals Kerala Ltd.	509.42	2588.73
	Ceramics & Refractories		
16.	The Chalakudy Refractories Ltd.	134.47	154.14

17.	Kerala Clays & Ceramic Products Ltd.	1.82	5.88
	Wood Based Industries		
18.	Forest Industries (Travancore) Ltd.	17.74	19.74
19.	Kerala State Wood Industries Ltd.	170.00	208.66
	Traditional Industries		
20.	Handicrafts Development Corporation of Kerala Ltd.	139.12	145.27
21.	Kerala State Coir Corporation Ltd.	119.31	161.03

Status of SLPEs in Kerala

The Table 7.2 presents the status of SLPEs as on March 31st 2004.

TABLE 7.2

Status of SLPEs in Kerala

Kerala

Years / *Items*	*1998-99*	*1999-00*	*2000-01*	*2001-02*	*2002-03*	*2003-04*
1. Total no.of SLPEs	111	111	112	111	113	113
2. No.of Working SLPEs	98	98	98	98	96	92
3. No.of Non-Working SLPEs	13	13	13	13	17	21
(i) Under Liquidation	6	6	6	6		
(ii) Under Closure	7	7	7	7		
(iii) Under Merger				--		
(iv) Others				--		
4. Total Equity	2954.01	3083.66	3281.06	3362.63	3325.06	3346.42
5. Total Debt	4775.74	5329.50	6023.46	6960.62	7496.64	8429.83
6. Total Investment	7729.75	8413.16	9304.64	10323.25	10821.70	11776.25
7. No.of Profit making enterprises	43	40	36	34	38	36
8. No.of Loss making enterprises	60	62	62	59	75	77
9. Net Profit/Loss	-51.12	-1.46	-195.1	-80.70	-100.38	-146.88
10. Accumulated Loss(-)/Profit	-1009.61	-1250.22	-1350.28	-1799.10	-1896.57	-2134.46

(*Source:* Reports of the Comptroller and Auditor General of India(Commercial),on Kerala for 1998-99 to 2003-04)

8

Management of State Level Public Enterprises of Orissa

R.K. Mishra, & R. Nandagopal***

[The purpose of this paper is to discuss the genesis, objectives, investment, patterns of organisation control systems boards of management and financial performance of the State Level Public Enterprises (SLPEs) in Orissa. The suggestions to effect improvements in the working of these PEs follow suit.]

Orissa is one of the bottom-line states in the country. Its per capita energy consumption, agriculture growth, industrial production and rate of literacy is lower as compared to the national average. On the contrary it has plentiful mineral and water resources. The most important challenge faced by the State during the four decades of post-Independence era is stepping up the rate of growth in the region to overcome economic stagnation. In the pursuit of achieving this end the State Government has opted for PSE as a means of economic development. The investments in PEs as well as their number have registered phenomenal growth. But these enterprises have lagged behind in terms of financial performance, so

* Faculty Member, Institute of Public Enterprise, O.U. Campus, Hyderabad- 500007.

** Faculty Member. Institute of Public Enterprise, O.U. Campus, Hyderabad- 500007.

much so that despite the deployment of fresh doses of funds year after year the accumulated losses have not allowed the net worth to show an increasing trend.

Genesis

The present State of Orissa was born in 1936. Later on, after independence 26 feudatory states were merged with it. At the time of its formation the State had no enterprise in public or private sector. The private sector was very shy of taking risks. Thus the feudatory States opted for development through involving themselves in directly productive activities. The Mayurbhanj Textiles Ltd., and the Titagarh Tannery Ltd both established in the year 1943 were the first PEs in Orissa. The former was a joint undertaking where the State's share was 62 per cent in the share capital of the company while the latter was a departmental enterprise. On the eve of the First Five Year Plan there were eight SLPEs in the State. These enterprises originated during the Second World War period when India was a base for the supplies and recruitment for the Britishers. The SLPEs between 1936 and 1961 i.e., by the end of Second Five Year Plan period were set up as the departmental enterprises. By the end of March 31st 1961 the number of SLPEs were 24. The Department of Industries had the maximum of 14 enterprises under its control while the Departments of Agriculture and Animal Husbandry, Supply and Transport had three units each under their charge. Most of these enterprises were in the field of textile, leather, tiles, trading land reclamation and transport. Excepting the leather industry and transport the SLPEs in other fields sustained heavy losses. Many of the SLPEs had to be closed down on account of their being an unviable proposition for the State.

Growth

Undeterred by the poor show of the departmental enterprises the State Government reaffirmed its faith in the SLPEs by setting up more and more enterprises during the third plan period. Prior to the third plan period the State had set up two statutory corporations, viz., Orissa State Financial Corporation and Orissa State Warehousing Corporation.

Besides these four undertakings, there were a few pilot project companies in the field of small scale industries set up by the Government temporarily on an experimental basis in the underdeveloped regions of the states. They were set up with the State's participation of 90% of the share capital with the objective of handing them over to the private sector after they become economically viable. The scheme of the pilot project companies was discontinued in 1978.

The Third Plan Period heralded a new era for the growth of the SLPEs. The Government set up the Industries Development Corporation of Orissa in 1962 with the objective of starting and promoting industrial units and providing financial and technical assistance to other industries in the State. This was the first of its kind in the public sector in Orissa to help rapid industrialisation. Orissa State Electricity Board (OSEB) was formed in 1961 which took over the then electrical divisions and departmental agency for electricity which ceased to exist from that date. The Orissa Construction Corporation was established in 1962 to take up various construction works of the government on contract basis and Orissa Forest Corporation in the same year came up to explore the possibilities of profitable use of forest resources and to develop forest based industries. Orissa State Commercial Transport Corporation was formed in 1961 to transport iron ore from Daitary mines to Paradeep Port and for handling import and export of cargo of Paradeep Port on behalf of various government departments.

During the Fourth Plan Period four new undertakings were set up. The Industrial Promotion and Investment Corporation of Orissa Limited was established for financing and promoting medium and large scale industries. The Orissa Small Industries Corporation was incorporated for promoting and establishing small scale industries. The Orissa Lift Irrigation Corporation was established for the creation of irrigation potential through installation of lift-irrigation projects and the Orissa State Road Transport Corporation came into being to provide the improved road transport services to the people in the State.

The Fifth Plan Period witnessed a rapid expansion in the public sector units. Seven SLPEs were set up during this period in different fields such as Film Development, Leather Products, Handloom, Fishing, Textiles, Maritime, Chilka Area Development, Cashew Development.

The Sixth Plan Period gave a big boost to the PE Philosophy in the State. During the first half of the Sixth Plan, twelve new enterprises were formed. The different areas in which these enterprises emerged included television, electronics, bridge construction, textiles, industrial infrastructure, tourism, police housing and social welfare. In the Seventh Plan Period, one enterprise was set up in 1985 to promote the plantation development. As on March 31, 1986 there were thirty three SLPEs in the State. Annexure-I contains the list of these enterprises.

According to the nature of operations the 33 SLPEs could be divided in four categories viz., production, promotional and development, service and commercial enterprises. Table-8.1 shows the classification of these enterprises in terms of these operational groups.

The table shows that out of a total of eleven production enterprises, six enterprises were incorporated during the Fifth Plan Period and one enterprise each in the Third Plan and Seventh Plan Period. Similarly, a major number of developmental enterprises have come up during and after the Fourth Plan Period. In case of service enterprises, four were formed upto the end of Third Plan and only two enterprises have been incorporated during Fifth and Sixth Plans. There were three trading enterprises up to the end of the Third Plan Period and an equal number of enterprises emerged during Fifth and Sixth Plan Periods. A close scrutiny reveals that between the end of the Third Plan and beginning of the Fifth Plan a very small number of these enterprises were set up in comparison to other Periods. The first half of the Sixth Plan witnessed highest number of 12 corporations followed by 7 in the Fifth Plan. The percentage of production enterprises is highest followed by developmental enterprises and trading enterprises. It is found that there is a marked shift in favour of production enterprises as they are continuously on the increase in comparison to enterprises in the other category.

TABLE 8.1

Classification of SLPEs in Orissa

Plan Period	*Production enterprises*	*Developmental enterprises*	*Service enterprises*	*Trading enter prises*	*Total no. of enterprises*	*% of Total*
Upto the end of IInd Plan	--	1	2	2	5	15
IIIrd Plan	1	1	2	1	3	15
Annual Plans	--	--	--	--	--	--
IV Plan	--	3	--	--	3	9
V Plan	3	2	1	1	7	21
VI Plan	6	2	2	2	12	37
VII Plan	1	--	--	--	1	3
Total	11	9	7	6	33	100
Percentage	31.26	28.12	15.62	18.75	6.25	

Patterns of Organisation

Table 8.2 reveals that out of the 33 SLPEs there are 28

government companies and 5 statutory corporations. There is no departmental SLPE in Orissa. All production enterprises are operating as government companies.

TABLE 8.2

Nature of Operation	*Government Companies*	*Statutory Corporations*	*Departmental Organisations*	*Total*
Production Enterprises	11	--	--	10
Developmental Enterprises	7	2	--	9
Service Enterprises	5	2	--	5
Trading Enterprises	5	1	--	6
Total	28	5	--	30
Percentage of Total	85	15	--	100

The company form of organization has been preferred to Statutory Corporation and Departmental forms on account of several reasons. First, it allowed the State Government to expeditiously set up the SLPEs. Secondly, it facilitated the takeover of joint ventures in the public sector. Thirdly, it permitted the State Government to avail of the institutional finance. Fourthly, it enabled the SLPEs to get requisite amount of operational autonomy to conduct their day-to-day business. Of the five Statutory Corporations, three were set up by 1961 to take benefit of the Central legislations and derive advantages which could accrue by following suit. The Orissa State Road Transport Corporation was also set up in pursuance of this logic. The industrial infrastructure development corporations have been set up in a majority of the States in the form of government companies. The Statutory Corporation form seems to have been accorded in the case of Orissa to provide it a special status in view of its glaring backwardness. As stated earlier, the number of departmental enterprises was 25 in 1967. The total extinction of this form is responsible for the Government's decision of discontinuing pilot projects, the closure of departmentally run economic activities on account of their heavy loss-making and conversion of many such units into the company form of organisation to benefit from the institutional add Central Government finance.

Objectives

Before independence Orissa had a very low level of industrialisation. It had only one sugar factory, one soap factory and a few other mills. The process of industrialisation could not pick up even during the First Plan Period in spite of the Government's policy of encouraging private enterprises through providing assistance in the form of land, power and raw materials. The Government therefore decided to accelerate the pace of economic development by setting up the SLPEs charged with the responsibility of achieving the following objectives:

- (i) Rapid industrialisation of the economy
- (ii) Reduction of regional imbalances;
- (iii) Provision of infrastructural facilities to attract private industrialists;
- (iv) Exploration of mineral and natural resources; and
- (v) Earn sufficient profits to plough back for further investment.

Investment

From an amount of Rs. 38.12 lakhs , on the eve of the First Five Year Plan, the investment in the SLPEs has shot up to Rs. 1076.38 crores in 1985-86. This comprised the investment by the State Government towards paid-up capital and loans of Rs. 439.04 crores which was 40.79 per cent of the total investment. The State Government's investments in equity of these enterprises has been increasing whereas the contribution towards the loans has been decreasing year after year. The debt-equity ratio is heavily weighed against these enterprises. The debt-equity ratio was 5.39:1 in 1983-84, 5.16:1 in 1984-85 and 4.79:1 in 1985-86. Out of the total investment by the Government as paid-up capital, investment in five undertakings, viz., Orissa Mining Corporation, Industrial Development Corporation of Orissa, Orissa Lift Irrigation Corporation, Industrial Promotion and Investment Corporation of Orissa, and Orissa State Road Transport Corporation accounted for 66% during 1985-86. The loan capital invested in the Orissa State Electricity Board accounted for about 74 per cent of the total loan investment in the SLPEs during the year. Table 8.3 discerns data on investment in the SLPEs of Orissa and table 8.4 explains the profile of SLPEs of Orissa.

TABLE 8.3

(Rupees in lakhs)

	1983-84	*1984-85*	*1985-86*
Total Equity	12440.49	15779.63	18559.54
Total Loans	73755.31	81421.63	89038.15
Total Investment	86195.80	97211.26	07637.69
Debt-Equity Ratio	5,93:1	5.16:1	4.79:1
Total Equity of State Government	11744.01	15075.15	17859.06
Percentage of State Government's Share of Total Equity	94.0	95.5	96.0
Total Loans of State Government	23230.26	24725.35	26009.00
Percentage of State Government's Loan to Total Capital	31.5	30.4	39.2

Source: Planning and Coordination Department, Government of Orissa, Bhubaneswar, *Public Enterprises Profile*, 1985-86, (March, 1987, pp. 1-16.

Boards

The Boards of SLPEs in Orissa in a majority of the cases, are in the nature of policy ones. They are headed by whole-time Chairmen-cum-Managing Directors drawn from the Indian Administrative Service. The size of the boards vary from a minimum of five in the Orissa State Electricity Board to a maximum of 16 in the Orissa Agro-Industries Corporation.

TABLE 8.4

Profile of SLPEs in Orissa

Years / *Items*	*1998-99*	*1999-00*	*2000-01*	*2001-02*	*2002-03*	*2003-04*
1. Total no. of SLPEs	36	36	36	36	70	70
2. No.of Working SLPEs	--	--	--	--	36	35
3. No.of Non-Working SLPEs	--	--	--	--	--	--
(i) Under liquidation						
(ii) Under Closure						
(iii) Under Merger						
(iv) Others	--	--	--	--	34	35
4. Total Equity	2048.43	2154.37	2206.52	2217.85	2418.59	2201.20
5. Total Debt	5704.55	6188.84	6733.73	6849.90	9,759.96	10,093.14
6. Total Investment	7752.99	8343.22	8940.26	9067.75	12,178.14	12,294.34
7. No. of Profit making enterprises	12	13	11	14	12	15
8. No. of Loss making enterprises	18	13	13	10	23	20
9. Net Profit/Loss	-536.80	29.16	-79.92	202.59	-571.06	-571.06
10. Accumulated Loss(-)/Profit	-1220.54	-1132.27	-1209.61	-1219.63	-2668.97	-2668.97

Source: Reports of the Comptroller and Auditor General of India (Commercial), on Orissa for 1998-99 to 2003-04.

The Orissa State Electricity Board has a functional Board. The Orissa Agro-Industries Corporation and the Orissa State Road Transport Corporation have part-time non-officials as their chairmen. The boards are over-represented by the IAS officers[1] . Non-officials have a very insignificant representation on the Boards[2]. In the case of the Government companies the finance secretary and the Secretary of the Administrative Department are ex-officio members of the boards. This apart, a director of related department of the Government is also a member on the board. The Managing Director and Chairman of some of the SLPEs have an interlocking membership. The tenure of the members of the Boards have averaged less than two years.

Financial Performance

The data given in Annexure-II, pertaining to gross profits, net profits, accumulated loss, interest, investment, turnover and capital employed reveal the following major financial phenomena:

1. The turnover of capital employed was very low. For all the SLPEs taken together, this ratio was around 0.35:1 in 1985-86. This shows the SLPEs suffered from the malaise of a heavy over-capitalisation. The investment in fixed assets and working capital were far more than required.
2. The accumulated losses of the SLPEs were on the increase. As on March 31, 1986 the accumulated losses were to the tune of Rs. 131.49 crores. In other words, the SLPEs were faced with the decline of net worth year after year. This cautions us about their financial sickness.
3. The number of PEs incurring net losses is on the increase. Out of 33 enterprises studied, information for 8 enterprises is not available and 13 are incurring losses. The remaining 12 are making profits but their profits are far less than the magnitude of colossal losses registered by the loss making enterprises.
4. The gross profits of PEs as a percentage to sales are horribly low. This percentage was 4.5 in 1985-86. In other words, the cost of sales of these enterprises is very high. This shows that the cost consciousness lacks in the enterprises.
5. The interest coverage is frightfully thin. This is because the debt-equity ratio in these enterprises is very high. In the face of continuous loss-making the consequence of high debt-equity ratio could be disastrous for any enterprise. The interest payments for 1985-86 for the

SLPEs totalled approximately to Rs. 47 crores which was more than twice as much of the gross profits.

6. One of the reasons for the low growth of turnover in the SLPEs has been a long lag between the increase in the price of inputs and the revision of the final prices of the goods produced/services rendered by these enterprises.

On an investment of Rs. 1,076.37 in 1985-86 these enterprises should have earned a minimum of 15 per cent rate of return which could have amounted to Rs. 1600 crores in 1985-86. But instead of earning profits on huge investments these enterprises incurred a loss of Rs. 63.96 crores during 1985-86. In 1984-85 and 1983-84 the size of net loss was Rs. 24.14 crores and Rs. 7.74 crores, respectively. Thus, the SLPEs have reached a sorry pass. They must either mend their ways or fold-up themselves from the economic scene. Now we would make some suggestions to make them financially viable and organisationally sound.

Suggestions

The SLPEs have constantly engaged the attention of the State Government for the last 20 years. The Government in 1966 had invited B.R. Shenoy, an eminent economist, for a critical study of the working of the SLPEs[3]. The findings of the report were not published. A three-man Committee headed by P.S. Lokanathan was appointed by the Government in October, 1967 to examine the programme of work undertaken by the PEs and suggest ways and means to make them achievement-oriented. This Committee, after enquiring into the working of 6 undertakings, including the Industrial Development Corporation of Orissa, Orissa Mining Corporation and Orissa Finance Corporation, observed that the SLPEs were plagued with excessive capital outlay and characterised by centralisation of decision-making regarding recruitment, investment and management of working capital. The Committee identified the undue delay in the preparation of accounts and recruitment of executives through deputation as the other weak spots of the SLPEs. The Committee suggested greater autonomy and delegation of power from the Government down to the different corporate levels in the SLPEB, appointment of full-time Chairmen and Managing Directors, nomination of eminent persons from the private sector on the Boards and complete overhauling of the financial and administrative procedures. We are offering below some pointed suggestions to help the SLPEs rid themselves of the heavy accumulated losses and assume the role of effective business entities.

i) Mergers, Closure and Privatisation

As would be seen from Annexure-I, many SLPEs are duplicating certain functions. In the field of transport, there is more than one undertaking. Similarly, in the field of industrial promotion the Industrial Development Corporation of Orissa, Industrial Promotion and Investment Corporation are virtually competing for the same ends. The Orissa State Electricity Board and Orissa Power Generation Company are also a case in point. In the same manner, we can venture to suggest the merger of the Orissa Road Transport Company, Orissa State Road Transport Corporation and Orissa State Commercial Corporation. These enterprises are not monolithic entities and consequently the unwieldy size does not pose to be a problem.

The Orissa State Electricity Board and the Orissa State Road Transport Corporation have been incurring huge losses for the last 5 years. Together they incurred 50 per cent net loss of all the SLPEs. The Orissa Industrial Infrastructure Corporation, the Orissa Road Transport Company, the Orissa Construction Corporation, the Orissa State Commercial Transport Corporation, the Orissa Lift Irrigation Corporation, the Orissa Maritime Chilka Area Development Corporation, the Orissa Tourism Development Corporation have also emerged as chronic losers. In the face of such a circumstance it is surprising to note as to why the State Government has not thought about pruning their size and taking hard decisions about the closure of some of these undertakings. In the case of a few undertakings, merger might also be an appropriate palliative.

ii) Turn-around Strategy

Some of the enterprises, as seen from Annexure-II, have been incurring losses for the last 2-3 years. In such cases an intensive analysis of their operations need to be done and specific turn around strategies are required to be formulated in association with management consultants.

iii) Toning up the Operational System

The SLPEs should be given sufficient freedom to manage their day-to-day operations. In the case of large number of SLPEs, rules and regulations with regard to the recruitment, promotion and performance appraisal have been borrowed from their administrative departments. The purchase policies have also been tailored on the basis of the Government systems and procedures.

iv) Increase in Turnover

The SLPEs should use their capacities to the full; if required, they may diversify their production. The necessary financial accommodation for this purpose should be extended by the Government. One common weakness afflicting the growth of business of these enterprises has been a total lack of awareness about the marketing functions. The creation of a full fledged marketing department would go a long way to improve the business prospects of these units.

v) Professionalisation and Strengthening of the Top Management

As PEs are expected to earn profits and a large number of these enterprises are in the nature of manufacturing and trading enterprises and many of these enterprises are handling highly complex technologies, there is a need to staff them with professionals. We would even like to suggest that the posts of Chairmen and Managing Directors in these enterprises should be manned by professionals. Training and management development could also act as a contributing factor to the professionalisation. Suitable training plans should be devised covering the Board members, executives and shop-floor employees. Top management in these enterprises is weak also on account of bifurcation of the post of the Chairman and Managing Director. One way to tackle this problem effectively is to merge the post of Chairman and Managing Director in all the SLPEs. Looking at the size of these enterprises in terms of both investment and turnover, it would not be out of place to make such suggestions. Further, the number of official directors on the Boards could be reduced to a maximum of two. The other members of the Board should be non-officials and part-timers. There is no need to have full-time Directors on the Board. The tenure of the Board Members should be fairly long and the Chief Executive should get a reasonable time to perform, which could be a minimum of 5 years old a maximum of two terms extending to 10 years in all.

vi) Corporate Plan

The SLPEs should formulate their corporate plan, spelling out clearly their corporate mission, objectives, goals, targets and activities. This would enable the SLPEs in seeking closer cooperation from the workers and securing tacit acceptance of the Government of their plan of action for immediate and future periods.

vii) Central Restructuring and Linkage with Capital Markets

The debt-equity mix in the SLPEs needs to undergo suitable changes. Some of these enterprises which have been performing well during the last five years may be allowed to go to capital markets to raise funds by way of equity and debt. The Orissa State Warehousing Corporation. Orissa Mining Corporation. Orissa Construction Corporation, the Orissa Forest Corporation and the Industrial Development Corporation of Orissa could be told to do this.

Conclusion

In pursuance of the economic policy of the Government, the SLPEs have proliferated in different fields of economic activity in Orissa. The salient features of their growth are that the number of production and manufacturing public enterprises is on the increase and the departmental form of PEs has given way to the statutory Corporation and Government company forms. The tempo of increase in investment has not been matched by the rate of return on the resources invested. The accumulated losses have been increasing year after year; so much so that they have led to the decline of the net worth in the SLPEs over the last four decades. This financial downturn could be arrested by drawing up suitable turn around plans, professionalising the PE cadres, strengthening the Boards of management of these enterprises and taking hard decisions with regard to their closure, merger and privatisation.

REFERENCES

1. Roy, R.C. *State Public Enterprise in India.* Uppal Publishing House, New Delhi, 1985, pp. 77-112.
1. Padhi, A.R. Working of State Enterprises in Orissa, in Khan. Ziauddin and Arora. Ramesh, K. (Ed.). *Public Enterprises in India.* Associated Publishing House, New Delhi, 1975, pp. 79- 92.

2. Sarma, R.P., *Investment Pattern of Public Undertakings in India: A Study of Orissa Enterprises*, Mittal Publications, Delhi, 1987, p. 23.
3. Kar, N.C., *A Study of Industrial Development Corporation of Orissa Ltd., as a State Enterprise*, M.Phil. Thesis, Utkal University, Bhubaneshwar, 1983.
4. Planning and Coordination Department (Government of Orissa, Bhubaneshwar), *Public Enterprises Profile 1985-86*, March 1987.

9

Development and Performance of State Level Enterprises in Punjab

*S.L. Kapur**

[This paper discusses the objectives, organisational forms, modes of control, capital structure, boards of management, financial performance and problems of the State Level Public Enterprises in Punjab.]

Introduction

This subject of State Level Public Enterprises have given due consideration, especially of their development and performance, to be very important, because in the national controversy which has now arisen, reference is seldom made to the circumstances in which, and the reasons why the concept of the Public sector as the main instrument of economic development was introduced. Another important factor to be considered is that whereas many studies have been done on central enterprises by individual researchers, independent institutions and Government bodies, studies on State Level Public Enterprises have been conspicuous by their negligible number. During the period of planned national growth State Level Public Enterprises have assumed considerable

* Financial Commissioner (Public Relations), Government of Punjab, Chandigarh.

importance. Even though they have not grown to the same extent as the Central Public Enterprises.

I believe an appropriate appraisal of the Public Enterprises requires consideration of the rationale of the public sector as originally conceived and assessment of its successes and failures over the last 35 years. This brings us to the genesis of the Public Sector.

The genesis of the Public Sector can be traced to the Freedom Movement, more than a decade and half before Independence, when at the Karachi Session of the Indian National Congress, Mahatma Gandhi moved the resolution of Fundamental Rights, which inter alia provided for "control by the State of key industries and ownership of mineral resources". A statement on industrial policy was made by Lord Wavell in 1945 prescribing that all ordnance factories, public utilities, railways and basic industries of key importance should be nationalised. The Government of India observed that, a free enterprise abroad or no free enterprise abroad, 'laissez faire' abroad or no' laissez faire' abroad in India, if progress is to be achieved, the development of industry must be planned by Government in cooperation with industry". In the post-independence era the thinking behind the public sector was conceptualised in the Industrial Policy Resolution, 1948 as modified in 1956, and the resolution passed by the Lok Sabha in December, 1954 adopting "socialistic pattern of society" as the objective of our development.

It was on the basis of the above-mentioned policy that the Second Five Year Plan was formulated, and it was the Second Five Year Plan that laid the foundation of Public Enterprises in India.

As far as the setting up of State Enterprises is concerned, there is neither a separate policy as in the case of Central Enterprises, nor a separate Act (like the Public Enterprises

Act) for the purpose. It is, however, true that the State Government have generally followed the policy of the Central Government in setting up State Enterprises. I believe the time has now come to rethink about the organisation, expansion and areas of operation for State Government Enterprises in view of the latest national thinking and the requirement of various states.

In the pre-Independence era, some of the princely States in Punjab used to operate a few State Enterprises, mainly to distil and distribute liquor. Some utilities supplying water and electricity were also there in the erstwhile East Punjab. The State Enterprises were run as departmental undertakings and not as companies, statutory or non-statutory. Immediately after the partition of the country, Punjab Roadways was started as a departmental undertaking. In order to promote faster economic development in accordance with the national policy, and for achieving other socio-economic objectives, the public sector was assigned an important role by the State.

The utilities were followed by institutions for providing infrastructure facilities for the development of industry and agriculture. Financial institutions, industrial estates, corporations for promoting the production and marketing of agricultural out-put were established by the Government. Punjab Financial Corporation was incorporated in 1953 under S.F.C Act, 1951 to work as a primary term-lending institution in the State and to help in its industrial development. Pepsu Road Transport Corporation was set up jointly by the State and the Central Government in 19-56 as a statutory body.

There were seven Corporations on November 1, 1966, the date on which the State was re-organised in its present form. These Corporations were expected to encourage industrialization, re-dress regional imbalances, exploit local resources, generate employment and develop technical man-power or in other words were supposed to promote growth and development with social justice. They were also charged with the responsibility to generate resources for the State Exchequer through efficient functioning on sound commercial lines.

After the reorganisation, the establishment of public enterprises became rather popular. One important reason was the direction received from the Central Government for converting departmental undertakings into Government companies and corporations to avail of capital participation by, or on behalf of, the Central Government and institutional finance. Another reason was that the setting up of a new corporation was thought to be the way out of the political embarrassment appeared to be caused by the continuous neglect of a sector. No sooner that, a decision was taken to set up a public corporation, the news was splashed widely through publicity media and an illusion was created which suggested that the new corporation would be a panacea for all ills in the particular sector. Successive Governments encouraged this belief. As a result, the number of enterprises mushroomed to 25 in 1980, and 28 on March 31, 1982. Out of these, ten are statutory corporation/companies as per the following statement.

List of Statutory Companies on 31st March, 1985

1. Punjab Financial Corporation.
2. Punjab State Warehousing Corporation.
3. Punjab State Electricity Board.
4. Punjab Scheduled Castes Land Development and Finance Corporation.
5. Punjab Backward Classes Land Development and Finance Corporation.
6. Punjab Women and Children Welfare and Development Corporation.

7. Pepsu Road Transport Corporation
8. Punjab Housing Development Board
9. Punjab Water Supply and Sewerage Board.
10. Punjab Ex-service Corporation.

Besides, there were 34 subsidiary companies or Punjab State Enterprises on that date. With the leasing out of Punjab Dairy Development Corporation to Milkfed (a cooperative), the number came down to 27 on March 31, 1985. There has been no change since then. The following tables, however, contain information regarding Punjab Dairy Development Corporation upto 9th April, 1983.

Financial Appraisal

Break-up of these enterprises, sector-wise, is as follows :

	Sector	Nos
1.	Primary Sector (Agricultural and Allied Activities)	6
2.	Secondary Sector (Industrial)	7
3.	Tertiary Sector :	
	(a) Financing (P.F.C)	1
	(b) Trading (PUNSUP)	1
	(c) Transport (PRTC)	1
	(d) Irrigation Sector :	2
	(i) Punjab State Electricity Board	
	(ii) Punjab State Tubewell Corporation	
(e)	Welfare Services	4
(f)	Other Services (including Punjab Dairy Development Corporation)	6

The investment of the State Government in the equity of these enterprises increased from Rs. 11,275.52 lakhs as on 31st March 1982 to Rs. 12,990.07 lakhs as on 31st March 1983, Rs.14,048.31 lakhs as on 31st March 1984 to Rs. 16,007.75 lakhs as on 31st March 1985. The position of investment made during the last four years is given in table 9.1

TABLE 9.1

Investment Position

(Rs. in lakhs)

Share Capital Contribution	1981-82	1982-83	1983-84	1984-85
(a) By State Government	11,275.52	12,990.07	14,048.31	16,007.75
(b) By others	1,369.54	1,801.57	2,150.12	2,426.93
Total	12,645.06	14,791.64	16,198.43	18,434.68

Besides, Loans amounting to Rs. 1,46,315.31 lakhs given by the State Government were outstanding as on 31st March, 1985.

The top six corporations/ Boards with reference to investment is given in table 9.2

TABLE 9.2

Top Six Corporations /Boards

(Rs. in lakhs)

	Equity	*Loan*	*Total*
(A) As on 31st March, 1983			
1. Punjab State Electricity Board	..	1,21,558.00	1,21,558.00
2. Punjab State Civil Supplies Corporation	373.00	19,662.00	20,035.00
3. Punjab State Tubewell Corporation	2,395.77	10,396.71	12,692.48
4. Punjab State Industrial Development Corporation	2,982.00	2,565.26	5,547.26
5. Punjab Financial Corporation	596.62	3,840.32	4,436..94
6. Pepsu Road Transport	2,450.95	1,002.64	3,453.59
Total	**8,798.34**	**1,59,024.93**	**1,67,823.27**

(B) As on 31st March, 1984				
1.	Punjab State Electricity Board	..	1,45,301.00	1,45,301.00
2.	Punjab State Civil Supplies Corporation	89.00	21,522.00	21,611.00
3.	Punjab State Tubewell Corporation	2,523.77	13,173.59	15,697.36
4.	Punjab State Industrial Development Corporation	3,282.00	2,911.23	6,193.23
5.	Punjab Financial Corporation	692.62	4,450.42	5,147.04
6.	Pepsu Road Transport Corporation	2,996.32	984.78	3,981.10
	Total	**9,587.71**	**1,88,343.02**	**1,97,930.73**
(C) As on 31st March, 1985				
1.	Punjab State Electricity Board	...	1,66,975.00	1,66,975.00
2.	Punjab State Civil Supplies Corporation	373.00	28,788.00	29,161.00
3.	Punjab State Tubewell Corporation	2,714.77	19,042.21	21,756.98
4.	Punjab State Industrial Development Corporation	3,682.50	3,268.56	6,951.06
5.	Punjab Financial Corporation	798.62	5,010.99	5,809.61
6.	Pepsu Road Transport	3,782.17	1,105.98	4,888.15
	Total	**11,351.06**	**2,24,190.74**	**2,35,541.80**

Overall Performance

The number of Corporations having earned profit was 13 in the year 1981-82 whereas it became 11, 11 and 1 in the years 1982-83, 1983-84 and 1984-85, respectively.

The Punjab State Leather Development Corporation and Punjab Ex-servicemen Corporation showed profits to the tune of Rs. 0.13 lakhs and Rs. 2.43 lakhs respectively during the year 1984-85 for the first time.

Tentative figures of profits earned / loss suffered in the years 1981-82, 1982-83, 1983-84 and 1984-85 are indicated in Table 9.3.

TABLE 9.3

Profit/Loss Position in Public Enterprises in Punjab

(Rs. in lakhs)

Sl. No	*Name of Corporation*	*1981-82*	*1982-83*	*1983-84*	*1984-85*
	(A) Profit earned by -				
1.	Punjab Financial Corporation	96.29	133.46	149.68	Loss
2.	Punjab State Industrial Development Corporation	162.47	81.56	71.82	92.80
3.	Punjab Small Industries and Export Corporation	20.16	20.71	3.38	37.14
4.	Punjab State Electronics Development and Production Corporation	0.14	0.31	Loss	1.01
5.	Punjab State Leather Development Corporation	Loss	Loss	Loss	0.13
6.	Punjab State Seeds Corporation	Loss	Loss	0.37	Loss
7.	Punjab Land Development and Reclamation Corporation	34.58	40.92	5.48	3.25
8.	Punjab Agro Industries Corporation	00.27	Loss	Loss	Loss
9.	Punjab State Warehousing Corporation	36.20	75.38	78.83	217.60
10.	Punjab State Forest Development Corporation	Set up in	1983	00.03	0.29
11.	Punjab Scheduled Caste Land Development and Finance Corporation	8.7911.97	9.48	12.02	
12.	Punjab Backward Classes Land Development and Finance Corporation	--	--	--	0.72
13.	Punjab State Civil Supplies Corporation	47.52	58.21	--	--
14	Punjab Housing Development Board	29.68	--	0.72	1.74
15	Punjab Water Supply and Sewerage Board	73.93	10.19	1.45	--
16	Punjab Dairy Development Corporation	92.25	12.34	--	--
17	Punjab Ex-Servicemen Corporation	--	--	--	2.43
	Total Profit (A)	602.37	445.05	348.24	369.13

(B) Loss suffered by -					
1.	Punjab Financial Corporation	--	--	--	-18.76
2.	Punjab State Electronics Development and Production Corporation	--	--	-0.09	--
3.	Punjab State Handloom and Textile Development Corporation	-14.44	-5.02	-5.39	-11.05
4	Punjab State Leather Development Corporation	-3.41	-6.55	-4.35	--
5.	Punjab State Hosiery and Knitwear Development Corporation	-14.65	-15.82	-22.59	-5.15
6.	Punjab State Seed Corporation	-0.64	-25.63	--	-68.03
7	Punjab Agro Industries Corporation	--	-42.16	-55.41	-92.94
8	Punjab Horticulture Corporation	-0.75	-2.93	-2.78	-1.19
9	Punjab State Tube well Corporation	-201.02	-98.55	-138.24	-379.60
10.	Punjab Backward Classes Land Development and Finance Corporation	-2.76	-1.20	-5.01	--
11	Punjab Women and Children Development and Welfare Corporation	-5.26	-9.93	-18.35	-23.95
12.	Punjab State Civil Supplies Corporation	--	--	-503.55	-1350.79
13.	Pepsu Road Transport Corporation	-736.41	-861.74	-1189.95	-1339.08
14.	Punjab Housing Development Board	--	-29.27	--	--
15	Punjab Water Supply and Sewerage Board	--	--	--	--
16	Punjab Tourism Development Corporation	-23.50	-36.67	-30.87	-35.43
17.	Punjab Film and News Corporation	-9.07	-8.51	-8.83	-8.90
18.	Punjab Poulty Development Corporation	-23.45	-14.16	-27.55	-10.96
19.	Punjab Ex-servicemen Corporation	-2.46	-2.33	-2.60	--
	Total Loss (B)	-1,037.82	-1,159.87	-2,015.56	-3,407.61
	Total Profit (A)	-602.37	445.05	348.24	369.12
	Net Profit / Loss	-435.45	-714.82	-1,667.32	-3.038.49

The top five corporations /Boards with reference to profit earned during the years 1981-82, 82-83, 83-84 and 1984-85 :

TABLE 9.4

List of Profit earned Corporations

(Rs. in lakhs)

Sl. No.	*Name of the Corporation*	
	1981-82	
1.	Punjab State Industrial Development Corporation	162.47
2.	Punjab Financial Corporation	96.29
3.	Punjab Dairy Development Corporation	92.25
4.	Punjab Water Supply and Sewerage Board	73.93
5.		
	1982-83	
1.	Punjab Financial Corporation	133..46
2.	Punjab State Industrial Development Corporation	81.56
3.	Punjab State Warehousing Corporation	75.38
4.	Punjab State Civil Supplies Corporation	58.21
5.	Punjab Land Development and Reclamation Corporation	40.92
	1983-84	
1.	Punjab Financial Corporation	149.68
2.	Punjab State Warehousing Corporation	78.83
3.	Punjab State Industrial Development Corporation	71.82
4.	Punjab Small Industries and Export Corporation	30.38
5.	Punjab Scheduled Castes Land Development and Finance Corporation	9.48
	1984-85	
1.	Punjab State Warehousing Corporation	217.60
2.	Punjab State Industrial Development Corporation	82.80
3.	Punjab Small Industries and Export Corporation	37.14
4.	Punjab Scheduled Castes Land Development and Finance Corporation	12.02
5.	Punjab Land Development and Reclamation Corporation	3.25

IV. DIVIDEND

Investment made by the State Government in the various Public Sector Undertakings as on 31st March, 1982, 1983, 1984, and 1985 in the shape of share Capital Contribution and Loans and the dividend and the interest received by the State Government is given in Table 9.5.

TABLE 9.5

Investment Position in State Level Public Enterprises in Punjab

Year	*Investment in the Equity Public Undertaking as on 31st March*	*Dividend received during the year*	*Percentage*	*Loans on Public Sector Undertaking as on 31st March*	*Interest received during the year*	*%age*
1981-82	11,274.52	..	..	86,553.38	476.85	0.55
1982-83	12,990.07	10.23	0.07	1,04,868.17	1,634.51	1.55
1983-84	14,048.31	35.27	0.25	1,24,047.40	1,697.83	1.36
1984-85	16,007.75	28.13	0.17	1,46,315.31	2,406.16	1.64

Though one of the objectives of the State participation in these undertakings is to promote growth in the fields where private capital is shy or is inadequate, yet return on investment made by the Government all along remained an important criterion for judging the performance of State Enterprises. The poor return of 0.17% has been the continuous concern of the State Government and efforts are being made to improve the performance of these undertakings in close cooperation with the Administrative Departments concerned. Although profit-making could not be the sole motive of public sector undertakings, yet there is no reason why these enterprises should remain a constant and continuous drag on the State Exchequer (Fourth Report on the Working of State Enterprises under print with State Government BPE Department of Finance).

Guarantee given by the State Government

State Government has not passed any law laying down the limit for giving guarantees. The Statement given below shows the guarantees given by the Government of Punjab for repayment of loans etc. raised by Statutory Corporations, Boards, local Bodies, Cooperative Banks/Societies and Rs. in Lakhs others and outstanding as on 31st March, 1982, 31st March, 1983, 1984 and 31st March, 1985.

TABLE 9.6

	1981-82		*1982-83*		*1983-84*	
	Sum Guaranteed	*Sum out-standing*	*Sum Guaranteed*	*Sum out-standing*	*Sum Guaranteed*	*Sum out-standing*
1. Statutory Corporation	2,45,72.77	1,91,54.34	3,32,95.00	2,20,05.97	4,10,63.69	2,82,06.25
2. Government companies	2,24,27.74	1,42,71.49	3,65,46.34	1,88,87.28	4,03,58.51	2,53,65.86
3. Local Bodies (including PWSSB)	50,54.54		21,87.99		39,48.22	
	40,27.07		21,57.87		31,86.84	
4. Private Companies	0.50	1.54	0.50	3.27	0.50	3.27

The profile of SLPEs of Punjab is given in the following table:

TABLE 9.7

Profile of SLPEs in Punjab

	Years					
Items	*1998-99*	*1999-00*	*2000-01*	*2001-02*	*2002-03*	*2003-04*
1. Total no. of SLPEs	53	53	53	53	55	64
2. No.of Working SLPEs	37	30	25	25	27	26
3. No.of Non-Working SLPEs	16	23	28	28	28	38
(i) Under Liquidation	3	8	1	14		

	(ii) Under Closure	6	6	5	4		
	(iii) Under Merger	--	--	--	1		
	(iv) Others	7	9	12	9		
4.	Total Equity	3349.24	3367.90	3390.55	3409.25	3,395.13	3432.78
5.	Total Debt	8262.84	9056.73	9464.85	9974.75	10,330	10350.33
6.	Total Investment	11612.08	12424.63	12855.40	13384.00	13,725.00	13783.11
7.	No.of Profit making enterprises	12	8	9	10	35	35
8.	No.of Loss making enterprises	24	27	23	25	29	29
9.	Net Profit/Loss	11.04	-104.86	-167.84	331.41	--	-90,126.40
10.	Accumulated Loss(-)/Profit	745.63	-846.57	1112.93	1434.68	--	-2,05,602.00

Source: Reports of the Comptroller and Auditor General of India (Commercial), on Punjab for 1998-99 to 2003-04.

Objectives and Evaluation

An analysis of the objectives of the State Enterprises shows the following categories of services provided:

(i) Utilities such as power, irrigation, water and transport.

(ii) Boards for meetings requirements of housing/sewerage.

(iii) Trading and service concerns for supply of physical inputs and services for industries and agriculture and for promoting experts.

(iv) Financing bodies for provision of credits for agricultural and industrial projects.

(v) Organisations for the economic uplift of a particular sector of the community.

(vi) Industrial development corporations for promoting new industrial projects and areas/townships and assisting existing industries.

(vii) Organisations for processing and distribution of agricultural products, milk, poultry etc.

(viii) Corporations for running cinemas, films, media activities and the like.

In keeping with the earlier thinking at the national level over-emphasis on the social role of the PSEs had caused confusion among the executives. For example when it came to providing employment development of ancillaries acquisition of technical know-how, location of a project they were told not to think in terms of profit. But in the end their performance actually was judged in the normal manner of profit and turnover etc., as in the private sector. At least this is the general impression generated by the various reports of the Government and the Committees set up to evaluate such enterprises including those constituted by the Vidhan Sabha.

Praxy Fernandes in his book *Promise and Performance* has described this phenomenon referred to above as "The dilemma which confronts the managements of Public Enterprises arises out of the multi-dimensionality of their goals and objectives. The organisations find themselves in a cleft stick serving so to speak- both god and Mammon, discharging both commercial and non-commercial objectives.

A group of experts meeting at Tangiers attempted to dissect the nature of public enterprises and proposed both statistical as well as conceptual definitions. It was the view of the group that the essence of the situation lay in a conscious acceptance that both the dimensions have a validity. (Report of the Expert Group Meeting on 'Concepts, Definition and Classification of Public Enterprises,' Tangiers, November, 1980). Clarity of objectives is very essential for evolving an appropriate system of evaluation. By now it is clear that any attempt to structure a uniform set of yardsticks for all public enterprises irrespective of their taxonomical situation would be an unrealistic pursuit. What can, however be attempted is to provide a basic framework for evaluative exercise and to adjust the specific questions needed to be posed to the situation of each enterprise. Fernandes hast in this context suggested the need to face two broad issues:

-- Why has the enterprise been created and what is its rationale and purpose?

-- Who is expected to pay for the cost of its goods and services?

I am in complete agreement with Praxy Fernandes that unless these two questions receive a clear and articulated answer. It is quite impossible to structure a system of performance evaluation. In Punjab, I notice, ambiguity surrounds these two questions and there is often a reluctance, due to reasons of political expediency or administrative inefficiency, to specify intentions. Therefore, the task of evaluation of Public Enterprises has become very complex. In the result everyone views public enterprises through his own eyes and judges these in relation to his own parameters.

I have noticed that new Corporations have been set up to perform in areas that should be very much the responsibility of the State for example developing markets, seed multiplication and distribution, scheduled caste and backward caste welfare, women's welfare etc. I believe these are the functions of the State's departments of agriculture and social welfare and should, therefore, be run departmentally. The argument put forward that run departmentally they will run inefficiently is not correct because as corporations they run just as inefficiently, particularly because they are run without the essential economic and commercial freedoms. [Report of the expert group meeting on 'Concepts, Definition and Classification of Public Enterprises', Tangiers, November, 1980.]

To cite an example, Punjab State Industrial Development Corporation (PSIDC), Punjab State Electronics Development and Production Corporation and Punjab Agro Industries Corporation are all promoting new industrial ventures in the public, joint and assisted sectors. In spite of the existence of specialised corporations, PSIDC is busy in setting new ventures in agro-industries and electronics, which is not justifiable. The objectives could be re-aligned to remove, or at least reduce, the overlap.

The Punjab Vidhan Sabha Committee on Public Undertakings in its Thirty-Second report, in respect of the general working of the Punjab Tourism Development Corporation (1983-84) had observed "that a reading of the objects contained in the Memorandum and Articles of Association of the Corporation shows that they have been copied mechanically from the Memorandum and Articles of Associations of similar organisations of other States without applying mind to the point whether they reflect Punjabi culture heritage socioeconomic life and religious and historical background. For instance, some of the objects like cabaret dance running breweries and distilleries etc. are irrelevant to the main functions of the Corporation and which in fact the Corporation may not be able to undertake". It was therefore recommended that the Corporation should immediately set up a Committee to draw the objectives anew so that those objectives which are unnecessary and irrelevant are deleted.

After a detailed and comprehensive study of the objectives of the various Punjab State Enterprises, I feel that the time is now ripe for a fresh calibration of the objectives of Public Enterprises to inject an element of dynamism, to ensure that scarce resources are not preempted through power at the expense of genuine need and to help base evaluation and accountability on well-known and pre-determined criteria.

In suggesting the following design of a new calibration, I have borrowed extensively from the views expressed by

Prakash Tandon in 'New Design for India's Public Sector' (*Mainstream*, May 30, 1987).

(a) The whole area of objectives should be carefully researched and studied for the distortions it has developed a new set of objectives evolved at the level of the units.

(b) In the annual commercial and social audit there should be an audit too of the objectives and their fulfillment and the deviations should be analysed to set the future course.

(c) The objectives should be primarily economic and the state and the society should find other institutional devices to perform non-industrial, non-banking and non-trading functions.

(d) Changes in objectives should be subjected to strict benefit-cost analysis, and any unviable growth should either be justified because of a long gestation or to achieve some technological breakthrough which has a risk attached.

(e) Over-lapping of objectives between various corporation has be avoided.

(f) Lastly, the objectives of an enterprise should be dynamic and change with time. but such change should be conscious, rational and not whimsical Controls

V. CONTROLS

The control over the Public Enterprises by the Legislature is operated through:

(i) Voting of funds.

(ii) Discussion on Annual Reports.

(iii) Statutory obligations.

(iv) Committee on Public Undertakings.

It is noteworthy that the State Legislature is beset with such limitations as lack of knowledge of its members, dependence on the Ministers for information, paucity of time, and restricted 'freedom' of its members to ask searching questions. It is generally alleged that questions are put by the legislators for political purposes. Likewise, debates usually go astray from the central subject under discussion. However, the Committee on Public Undertakings is playing a useful role. Nonetheless, this committee, having less than a specialised a character, performs only post Mortem functions and has insufficient time at its command to be able to cover all state enterprises under its jurisdiction even once in a span of three years.

The Administrative Department can issue directives to the Public Enterprises on policy matters. Generally speaking the boards of directors are wholly nominated by the State Government in the Administrative Department. These nominee directors, particularly those drawn from the Administrative Department, normally act as the main instruments of control over the boards and the chief executives. Besides, the Memorandum of Associations of the Enterprises usually reserve all important policy decisions for the Government. For instance the selection of the private promoter, for participation in a joint sector project with Punjab State Industrial Development Corporation is made by the Projects Approval Board, headed by the Chief Minister. Moreover, a considerable amount of ministerial control is exercised through personal and informal contacts between the Ministers, the Secretaries and the board members.

In addition, the Department of Finance has the power to determine the character and the quantum of capital investment. It also has the authority to nominate a director. The Bureau of Public Enterprises was set up in September, 1979 in the Finance Department to provide a central point of reference devise steps to increase profitability and review periodically the working of Public undertakings.

The audit of these enterprises is carried out by the Accountant General of Punjab and also by commercial auditors approved by the Accountant General. This takes a lot of time, besides falling short of the high standard of 'performance audit' or 'efficiency audit' as suggested by Ashok Chanda (Indian Administration London, 1958) for such enterprises. As a result we witness today the strange phenomenon of almost all state enterprises operating on the basis of tentative balance sheets.

Perhaps the most complex problem area in the administration of State Government enterprises concerns the difficulty of striking at a point of optimum balance between the control overt and autonomy oft these undertakings. There is no standard pattern of its; it varies from department to department. Generally the departments adopt a superior fatherly attitude trying to run the whole show. Autonomy of Punjab State Enterprises is reduced to a myth. In theory, on the other hand the public sector enterprises and their managements are responsible for actual performance and explanations are given by them for poor results- whether to the audit or to the public or to the Vidhan Sabha. Why not then define the respective roles and responsibilities more precisely?

A lot of literature has appeared on this subject. Personally I am attracted by two suggested control systems:

(a) The Corporate Planning Approach advocated by Praxy Fernandes.

(b) A Two-tier board system- Supervisory Board and a Managing Board - put forth by Prakash Tandon.

The Corporate Planning approach implies "that each public

enterprise will generate an internal process of examining its objectives, financial and social; its place in the national (State) developmental strategy, its investment, financial, production, materials, personnel and marketing plans, over a perspective period. These will then be incorporated in all integrated corporated plan including within it the predetermined yardsticks of performance evaluation. The Corporate Plan would then be negotiated with the Government on the French lines and after approval would provide the enterprise with a clean mandate". (Praxy Fernandes: Promise and Performance: P.103) While proposing a new design for India's Public Sector (*Mainstream* May 30, 1987) Prakash Tandon has interalia suggested the concept of a two-tier board. The Managing Board will plan, implement and act, and will be responsible to the Supervisory Board who will appraise and approve. This two-tier board is an integral part of a total new systems and legislation approach suggested by him for the public sector. As it may not be possible to put through this new package deal in the immediate future, as a short-term strategy, we may have to adopt the suggestion made by Fernandes. L.K. Jha has similarly suggested in his book: "Economic Strategy for the 80s".

Regarding timely completion of audit, I will commend creation of new audit structures for the prompt conduct of financial as well as performance audit of State Public Enterprise. If required, a national level initiative any be taken by the Union Minister of Public Enterprises in this behalf.

VI. INTERNAL MANAGEMENT SYSTEMS

The public enterprises in Punjab today are understandably structured and shaped in the image of those that spawned there, namely, the administration. An interesting and equally irrelevant concomitant of the administrative structure is the sanctioned strength" system for staff recruitment, whereby secretarial, clerical and service staff is employed not to serve a functional need but as a hierarchical appendage.

B.S. Khanna and Sudesh Kumar Sharma found, on analysis, two patterns of hierarchy in Punjab. Out of the 11 Punjab Public Undertakings that they studied, nine fell in category A and only two in Category B, (*Public Sector Undertaking in India:* Ziauddin Khan and Ramesh K. Arora).

Category A

B.O.D

Chairman OR M.D.C

Financial officers	Secretary	Technical officers
Field Agencies	Establishment	Field Agencies
	Category B	
	B.O.D	
	Chairman OR M.D.	
	Secretary	

Office Staff Technical Officers

They also reviewed the hierarchy of the administrative set-up of several of the public undertakings in Punjab and opined that the span of control with the organisations was weak.

Plans

Most of the Public Enterprises prepare their Five-Year Plans which are dovetailed into the Five Year Plan of the State Government. I have had an occasion to go through some of these plans and I find that these have been framed with expertise and professional skills. For instance, Punjab State Industrial Development Corporation (referred to as Punjab State Industrial Development Corporation PSIDC) had prepared a plan envisaging:

(a) A total requirement of Rs. 86.50 crores in the Plan period (1985-90)

(b) A total investment of Rs. 38.50 crores in projects to be completed within the plan period. These projects would entail a total capital outlay of Rs. 667 crores and generate employment for about 22000 persons.

For term lending, Punjab State Industrial Development Corporation prepares a Business Plan and Resources Forecast which is approved by the Industrial Development Bank of India as well as by the B.O.D.

Internal Audit

The enterprises have set up internal audit structures. There are some corporations like the PSIDC which have their own accounting manuals for exercising control. PSIDC is also getting its internal audit done by a firm of chartered Accountants. On the other hand, there are some corporations like Punjab State Small Industries Corporation Limited, where Internal Audit, instalied in 1980 in the shape of a separate wing, is reportedly not working according to any rule or procedure. The Committee on Public Undertakings had to comment adversely on this aspect in its Thirty-Sixth Report (1987).

M.I.S. and other Management Devices

All the enterprises have installed M.I.S. in some form or the other. Punjab State Electricity Board, Punjab Finance Corporation and Punjab State Industrial Development Corporation all reportedly having the best systems. The major activity of PSIDC is on the project promotion and term-lending. Its M.I.S was studied. It has developed a format in which information is collected for projects in operation and those under implementation. These formats are given in Appendix IX. Punjab State Industrial Development Corporation is one of the few companies which is also using a computer to keep its information upto date and to analyse it quickly.

The managements are generally aware of the advances in management culture and evolution of new management techniques, tools and aids. The Electricity Board, the Punjab State Industrial Development Corporation and a few other progressive Corporations are extensively using these new techniques. On the other hand, there are "corporations like Punjab Film and News Corporation which have not so far used many of the modern management techniques to optimise performance.

Monitoring

Pepsu Road Transport Corporation, Punjab State Electricity Board, Punjab State Industrial Development Corporation and Punjab Financial Corporation are some of the enterprises which believe and act on the principle that monitoring of projects and performance is very important. Scientific management and maximisation of efficiency have placed the Punjab Financial Corporation in the category of one of the best State Financial Corporations in the country, particularly in the field of monitoring of loans. The corporation has set up a properly manned Monitoring Division. Similarly, Punjab State Industrial Development Corporation has a Monitoring Division which also assists its nominee directors by examining agenda papers. These directors represent Punjab State Industrial Development Corporation interests as a promoter or as a term lender on the Boards of assisted companies.

Financial Administration

An analysis of the functioning of the Public Enterprises under study indicates that the principle of financial autonomy of the undertakings has yet to be adequately recognised by the Punjab Government. The State Finance Department is also generally averse to delegating responsibilities for financial scrutiny and evaluation of proposals for capital investment to the board of directors of these corporations (Public Enterprises in India: Ziauddin Khan etc).

The enterprises have, however, accepted the recommendation of the Public Undertakings Committee, contained in its 1st report, and have framed financial rules and procedures. However, the existing practice of preparing the balance-sheet appears to be inadequate for effective management control. If financial reporting is properly organized, the task of audit becomes substantially simple, and the accountability requirements can be met better (S.K. Chakraborti, "Appraisal of Management Environment and Imperatives" *Indian Journal of Public Administration*, April-June 1971 p. 67).

The Enterprises are continuously striving to evolve better pricing and purchase policies in the interests of better performance.

An analysis of capital structure of Public undertakings in Punjab reveals that the proportion of equity capital is somewhat larger than the loan capital (*Public Enterprises in India:* p. 122). Restructuring of the capital base is thus called for to optimise performance of the undertakings.

Boards of Directors

The Punjab Government has been rather shy of setting up statutory corporations out of the 27 public sector enterprises this form has been adopted in the case of ten only. The reason seems to be that the State Government, having little confidence in the viability and the managerial autonomy of the corporation form as a preference for the company form or organisations so as to be able to retain a comprehensive control over the undertakings (Ziauddin Khan etc. Public Enterprises in India p. 96).

In the 27 Punjab State Enterprises under study, policy-making boards (i.e. Boards, the Members of which than the chief executive, are part-time) operate in 26. The Electricity Board is the only enterprise which can be said to have a mixed board having both part-time and whole-time directors.

It is noteworthy that in all such enterprises, the boards of directors are nominated by the State Government. Except in the case of State Electricity Board and the Punjab Financial Corporation, no qualifications are prescribed for the directors Proper control and good management are the two objectives apparently kept in view by the State Government while nominating the directors. The government generally nominates its higher administrative officers as directors of enterprises. Nowadays 24 out of the 27 enterprises are headed by I.A.S. officers. 20 out of these 24 part-time chairmen are also the Administrative Secretaries concerned. Except for some of the statutory boards like Electricity Board the other part-time directors are also generally drawn from the I.A.S. cadre; more than 50% of such directors belong to this service. During the period of elected Government MLAs and other political supporters were also appointed as chairmen and directors. In fact, during the last Akali Government 18 of the chairmen were either sitting MLAs or party functionaries. They were nominated as such because they were important for the party and could not be accommodated in the cabinet and not because of any merit or ability connected with the working of the enterprise.

The Chief Executive

The Managing Director or General Manager is nominated by the Government. He is generally an officer taken on deputation from the administrative or technical cadres of the State. However, instead of making a careful selection based on an evaluation of the background and aptitude and subjecting the prospective appointee to intensive training in principles of business management in general and in the working of similar undertakings in particular, the State Government at present, in general, arbitrarily picks up one or the other person to fill the key executive positions. Besides, with changes in personal and political predilections and other subjective criteria, these executives are changed arbitrarily at rather short intervals before they can contribute to the sound and systematic working of the undertaking.

Meeting and Interface with Government

The B.O.D. normally meets 4-5 times a year. Many directors seem to have casual interest in the working of the corporations. The committee on Public Undertakings has observed in its Second Report that in most of the meetings of the Punjab Export Corporation, only two or three out of the 13 directors usually attended the meeting. By placing the Secretary as the Chairman, the problem of coordination between the Government and the B.O.D has been solved to a considerable extent.

Suggested Improvements

The Committee on Public Undertakings in its second report to the Punjab Vidhan Sabha made the following suggestions:

1. Utmost care should be taken in selecting top managers. They must not only be competent in doing the job with which they are entrusted but also capable of getting the best out of the men under their charge and of making them feel that they have a stake in the success of the enterprise in which they work.
2. There should be some arrangement in the Government for an independent and objective examination of matters coming from Corporations. In other words, the proposers and scrutinizers should not be the same.

3. The association of Secretariat officers on the board of directors should be minimised and non-official elements should be introduced on such boards.
4. Keeping in view the requirements of the tasks to be performed members of the board of directors should be drawn from a wider sphere than the present and more technical experts experienced men from public life and from various non-official sources should be appointed on the boards.

A lot of literature has been published on this subject. Various experiments have also been tried. The following suggestions are made on the basis of my comprehension and experience:

(a) The boards should be compact and the membership should not exceed ten in any case.

(b) On the lines of Government of India's policy, the chief- executive should be the Chairman-cum-managing director. Separate part-time chairmanship should be discouraged.

(c) Bigger companies should have more than one functional whole- time director.

(d) The C.M.D. and whole-time directors may be selected out of applications invited for specific posts. The selection has to be made carefully by a statutory public sector selections board (constituted on the lines of the PSEB). They should be given fixed tenures of 3-5 years. Government officers may be permitted to apply. They could be taken on deputation also. This has to be permitted because State Public Enterprises cannot at present attract many really talented people from outside the Government. Moreover, good Government officials may not be willing to give up their substantive posts for ever to join the enterprises.

(e) Political persons and MLAs need not be appointed on the boards in keeping with the recommendation of Administrative

(f) Reforms Commission and the practice followed in advanced democracies like U.K.

(g) Administrative Secretaries should not be directly associated with these boards. The number of direct Government nominees (to be drawn from the Administrative. Finance and other connected departments) should never exceed three.

(h) Not more than 2 public men, with requisite qualifications and background, may be appointed on each board.

(i) Certain general qualifications should also be prescribed for the members of the board; and

(j) While appointing part-time official nominees to the board Government should see that the persons so nominated do not have to serve on more than two or three boards and are not so burdened with their subsantive work that they find it difficult to playa useful part in board meetings.

Human Resources Management

Except for PSEB, PSIDC and a few other well managed enterprises, where some preliminary objective projections of manpower requirements are worked out, no scientific manpower planning seems to exist in any other State Enterprise. Reference has already been made to the concept of 'sanctioned strength of staff bodily lifted from the Government system and incorporated in the public enterprises structure. Most of the State Enterprises have acquired the typical "administrative ratio of teeth-to-tail in which a large irrelevant, non-specialised, under-worked staff tail is attached to an inadequate and small group of over-worked decision-makers, who consequently have little time to think, plan and evaluate." (New Design for India's Public Sector: *Mainstream*, May 30, 1987 p. 29).

Selection procedures and standards vary from corporation to corporation. Similarly, the terms of employment of the public sector personnel are characterised by their diversity. The senior level staff is generally on deputation from the Government. The orders for Development are issued by the C.M. in the General Administrative Department. There is very little evidence of a really perfect selection process for recruiting competent personnel in a just and equitable manner. It is a fact that the autonomy of the public enterprises in regard to recruitment, is constantly encroached upon by persons in authority who are themselves under pressure of an articulate middle class who hunger for employment. This feature has been well brought out by two Bangladesh economists, Rehman Sobhan and Muzaffar Ahmed (Public Enterprises in an Intermediate Regime: published by Bangladesh Institute of Development Studies, Dhaka) who have aptly termed the phenomenon as surplus extraction from public enterprises at the inter-mediate level. During the period of the elected Governments public corporations are used rather unashamedly to provide employment opportunities to the near and dear ones of the powers that be.

I studied PSIDC regarding its human resources development programme. The corporation has prescribed a regular training schedule for all levels of managers. In fact there is an annual training schedule drawn up while keeping in view the training needs determined in consultation with the divisional heads. Training programmes conducted by the various institutions of repute are utilised. There are some specialised programmes conducted by the financial institutions like IDBI. Reserve Bank of India etc. for which the concerned managers are deputed.

The Punjab State Industrial Development Corporation follows an enlightened promotion policy based on efficiency and performance. Performance evaluation is used for monitoring the work of individual managers. Senior Managers are paid well and in any case better than those of the Punjab Government. Non- management staff is in Government grades. 80% of the staff consists of professionals in various specialised fields like engineering, finance, accountancy, business management and the like. The Corporation has been able to build a professional cadre of managers who can be compared to the best in their respective fields. This is an exceptional development for the state enterprises and is a tribute to the sagacity and excellent work of a succession of Industries Secretaries and Managing Directors, who have striven hard to nurture this cadre.

Regarding deputation of Government staff, while there may be some justification for having Managing Director and other senior technical and administrative personnel on deputation, there cannot be any justification whatsoever for having middle and lower level staff on deputation. The Committee on Public Undertakings in its 38th report (1986-87), recommended that in future no clerical staff should be taken on deputation. The Committee also recommended in its 3rd report relating to the Punjab Tubewell Corporation, that the deputationists should be reverted or absorbed in the corporation within two years.

Recommendations

(a) A new staffing pattern has to be evolved for each enterprise. This pattern has to be need- and not culture-oriented and should be determined with the help of business and industry experts.

(b) PEs should be encouraged to develop their own cadres. Small enterprises in the same sector may join each other in having common cadres. Government servants should not normally be asked to fill in the gaps.

(c) These cadres should be trained and professionalised. Promotion policies should be oriented to the encouragement of efficiency, honesty and business and professional skills.

(d) A service selection board (preferably a statutory one) for selection of senior executives of these enterprises be set up. It could function along the lines of PSEB at the Centre.

(e) Punjab State Administrative Institute should be suitably strengthened to meet the training requirements of various state enterprises.

(f) Development of a fundamentally Indian Management approach to the issue of dealing with the Human Capital.

A new brand of Managers has to emerge who can motivate employees to contribute their minds as well as their work to the corporation, like they do in Japan; (Akio Morita : *Made in Japan*).

Optimum Size of a State Level Public Enterprises

Recent writings on the subject have indicated that institutional choices do matter a great deal in determining economic outcomes (Leroy P. Jones and Edward S. Mason: *Public Enterprises Sector in Less Developed Countries;* Cambridge University Press). Organisational failures are as innocent as market failures in explaining sub-optional economic performance. Economic factors explain a great deal of the observed size and structure of public enterprises. Leroy P. Jones has pointed out some other important sectors: for instance, Malaysia has established many Small Public Enterprises to help effective Malays. Bangladesh took over many Small

Public Enterprises after its liberation. Do we have a lesson in this for India ? Can we really lay down some criteria for determining an optimum size of a public enterprise ? For, if we can do that, we will be solving some of the more important problems which we face on account of multiplicity of corporations and setting up of some very small-sized ventures.

Some Interesting Features of the PSIDC

Having been a former Chairman of the PSIDC and retaining a lot of interest in industrial development of the State, I have tried to probe the present-day working of this Corporation. Some of the more interesting features are:

(a)·Investment Decisions

Being the promoter of industry in the large and medium sectors. PSIDC, through its project division identifies the project which can be set up in the State, keeping in view the availability of raw-materials technology, market for the product etc. Thereafter it procures Letters of Intent/Registrations from the Government of India and after following the set procedure, makes selection of the private financial collaborator for the joint sector projects and in collaboration with the joint sector partner makes the final investment decision. In the case of public sector such decisions are made by the PSIDC itself. In practice investment decision as well as the selection of private entrepreneur in the case of joint sector is simultaneous.

Although, technically, only the Project Approval Board decides about the private partner, it also indirectly approves the investment-decision considering the various aspects of the project like availability of raw materials, market technology, the employment potential and its relevance to the State economy.

In the case of term-lending activity there is a very detailed scientific appraisal of the project which looks into 'profitability. The background of the promoters, the technology, the market, the position of similar industries within the State and outside, overall reports of the all-India financial institutions like the Industrial Development Bank of India. If the project is found viable on its appraisal, it is placed before the Committee of Advisers which consists of the PSIDC's senior managers and outside experts. After this Committee's approval, the project is placed before the sub-committee of the Board to finally sanction the loan. The loan is further pre financed by the Industrial Development Bank of India.

(b) Location

Location of the project is based on the conditions of the Letters of Intent/Registrations. The Government of India encourages some projects only in the centrally declared backward areas of the State. Under the Punjab Government orders the location of every project is to be finally cleared by the Punjab Government in the Department of Industries. In the location of the project, the views of the private sector promoter, as also the foreign technical collaborator from whom the technology is obtained, are also kept in mind. As a direct consequence of the deteriorating law and order position in the State, the entrepreneurs are preferring the districts of Ropar, Hoshiarpur and Dera Bassi (sub-division of Patiala District) for locating new projects. Although both the PSIDC and the Punjab Government have been keen to promote industries in the border and other backward areas, there has been some resistance to such efforts from the entrepreneurs. But having said all this it is pertinent to mention that PSIDC's projects are located all-over the State and particularly in the backward and border districts of Gurdaspur, Ferozepur, Hoshiarpur, Sangrur and Bhatinda.

(c) Technology

The choice of technology has been made generally in consultation with the private parties in the case of joint sector projects and by the respective companies in the case of the public sector units. The search for technology is made through various sources after ensuring its appropriateness as well as availability. Of course, the final approval for acquisition of technology is always obtained from the Government of India. In most of the cases, PSIDC has obtained the most modern and appropriate technology; however, there have been a few instances in the initial stages of the Corporation's functioning when it could not get the most appropriate technology on account of lack of knowledge and experience. Most of the subsidiary companies have, however, updated their technology and have also established very good R & D teams for the purpose.

(d) Productivity

The productivity of the companies has been generally satisfactory. The subsidiary companies have generally been able to achieve a capacity utilisation of 75 to 80% in the third year of their production. Luckily, the labour relations in the companies have also been good. Proper selection systems and training, adoption of sound managerial practices, nurturing of an enlightened labour policy and the right choice of the technology, have optimised productivity.

(e) Augmentation of Resources

Punjab State Industrial Development Corporation disinvests in various companies after the projects get into production. This is generally done in favour of the joint sector partner. Normally the prices are par value of the share plus institutional rate of interest at the time of sale or market value, whichever is higher. During the year 1986-87, Punjab State Industrial Development Corporation mobilised an amount of Rs. 467 lakhs from disinvestments. The actual surplus out of this was Rs. 150 lakhs. Resources have also been obtained from dividends received in respect of some of the companies in which Punjab State Industrial Development Corporation invested. Again, the interest income derived from the assisted units is also an important source of funding. However, the main source continues to be the budgetary support received from the State Government.

(f) Decision-making

The joint sector promoter is approved by the Projects Approval Board but other policy decisions are taken by the Board of Directors of the Corporation. The Board has also adequate delegation in terms of sanction of loans and other matters relating to project promotion. Day-to-day management is looked after by the Managing Director who has been delegated powers in personnel matters like recruitment, in financial matters like sanctions and other relative areas. The decision-making has been adequately delegated in Punjab State Industrial Development Corporation. With the passage of time, more delegation may take place at the level of General Managers and Executive Directors.

Punjab State Industrial Development Corporation has generally retained its professional character.

XI. Conclusion

The State public sector has come of age; it has been nurtured by the State for 35 years. Some of the State public sector enterprises have done well. Others have not succeeded at all. The financial performance of the total sector is not very encouraging. On an over-all basis, it can be inferred that the enterprises have been drained upon the resources to which these should have been contributing. It should have been a model for industry in technology. Efficiency, innovation, productivity, and public interest; instead, it has limped in indifferent health. And yet to those of us who have worked in it, its problems are tractable.

I would like to suggest that this very institution should develop the subject of a New Design for the State Public Sector which would be suitable for 1990's and beyond.

One should be clear on its objectives, its structures of capital and the boards, the management, culture and linkages with the different sectors of society. This institute with the support of State public enterprises, could undertake a study to prepare a New Design.

10

Management of State Level Public Enterprises in Rajasthan

R.K. Mishra, & R. Nandagopal***

Rajasthan is one of the leading States in the country in terms of area, mineral resources, population and hidden potential for growth. One of the avowed objectives of the economic planning in the State has been to develop its different regions through the growth and expansion of public sector. In keeping with this strategy the State has invested a major chunk of its planned resources in the public sector. As a result, the number of public enterprises (PEs) and investments therein have increased phenomenally during the planned economic era. The financial performance of these enterprises has not been in tune with the expectations. The SLPEs in Rajasthan have come in for sharp criticism in the State Legislature, provincial and national press, academic and research forums. Their performance has become a matter of serious concern to the planners and policy-makers. The purpose of this paper is to assess the financial performance, of these enterprises and offer a framework needed to make them financially viable.

* Faculty Member, Institute of Public Enterprise, O.U. Campus, Hyderabad -500 007.

** Faculty Member, Institute of Public Enterpriset O.U. Campus, Hyderabad- 500007.

As a prelude, the paper outlines the genesis, objectives, growth, patterns of organisation and control structure of SLPEs in Rajasthan.

Genesis

The State of Rajasthan was carved out by integrating 19 princely States and 3 chief-ships. Most of the princely States were performing the functions of a welfare state. They were involved in developing industry, agriculture, banking and institutional structure for providing agricultural and industrial finance. Roads and Railways are the two most prominent means of transport in Rajasthan. Princely States of Sirohi, Mewar, Jaipur, Jodhpur and Alwar had developed a vast network of road. The state of Sirohi took the initiative of starting the road passenger transport services jointly with an individual in 1914.

The princely states took keen interest in the development of railways. The States of Jodhpur, Bikaner and Jaipur managed efficiently their railways and were categorised as the first class railway systems in the country. The railways were making profits and yielding sufficient surpluses. The rate of return varied between 4 to 8 per cent. The route mileage of railways in Bikaner, Jodhpur, Jaipur, Mewar and Dholpur States was more than 2,100 miles. The road mileage in the princely states was about 2,600 miles.

The princely States lacked the know-how in the field of minerals and mining. Despite this, their achievements were note- worthy. In the Jaipur State Lignite, Copper, Mica, Soap Stone, Gypsum, Marble, Zinc were mined on a considerable scale. The Bikaner State commenced its own regular mining of lignite and coal in 1898. The lignite mines had an impressive record of profits. The rate of net profit on capital in the year 1904-05 was in the vicinity of 15 per cent. The manufacture of salt was undertaken by the States of Udaipur, Bikaner, Jodhpur,

Jaipur, Alwar, Bharatpur and Dholpur. The princely State of Jodhpur administered this industry through a separate department. The department was staffed with trained and efficient officers. The officers were given a long tenure. The princely states, in order to make the industry operations business-like, introduced on the job training and monetary incentives for good work. The princely state of Bharatpur had set up agricultural credit banks to help the farmers. However, this experiment did not turn out to be a success.

The princely state of Bikaner had set up a State Savings Bank in 1927-28. The Kishangarh State set up an industrial finance bank to rejuvenate the old and declining industries.

The princely states did not make great strides for setting up of large scale industries. The dearth of finance was the major inhibiting factor. However, they operated cotton presses and ginning factories, glass works, timber factories and hotels.

Thus, it is clear that Public Enterprises spurred the economic prosperity in the princely states. They were run on the principle of making profits and organised in the departmental form. Their performance was assessed regularly by the prime ministers of the princely states, and only in exceptional cases the issue pertaining to them were put before the rulers. The productivity of labour was high and the system of punishment and reward was in vogue.

Growth, Objectives, Investment and Patterns of Organisation

The number of Public Enterprises in Rajasthan shot up from one in 1955 to 36 in 1985. These Public Enterprises have been entrusted with activities varying from provision of industrial and agricultural finance to the construction of bridges and production of salt and sugar. The growth of Public Enterprises could be studied in time phases, viz., the period of transition, the era of expansion and proliferation and the stage of consolidation. From 1941 to 1954, the State Level Public Enterprises were in the transitory phase. Immediately after the formation of Rajasthan, the enterprises owned and managed by the princely states such as railways, sulphate and salt works were taken over by the Central Government. The State Government was not upset by the setback as it had been very keenly observing the process of economic development under way in the other parts of the country and the economic philosophy of the Centre. As a result, while formulating policy for the economic growth of the State, heavy emphasis was placed on the setting up and expansion of the State Level Public Enterprises.

This in turn led to the establishment of 32 public sector units over the period 1956-79. During this period between 1956 and 1961, 7 enterprises were set up. Most of these enterprises were transferred from either the Centre or taken over from the private sector. The Rajasthan State Electricity Board a major State Level Public Enterprise came into being in 1951. These enterprises were of development and manufacturing nature. From 1961 to 1966, six units were set up. These units were in the nature of service development and manufacturing enterprises. The Rajasthan State Road Transport Corporation was set up in 1964. The years 1969-74 were marked with striking innovations. The Rajasthan Housing Board, the Rajasthan State Agri-Industries Corporation the Rajasthan State Industrial Development and Investment Corporation Rajasthan Tribal Area's Development Co-operative Federation and Rajasthan State Tanneries were set up during these years. The years 1974-79 led to the establishment of 11 Public Enterprises which included the Rajasthan State Mineral Development Corporation, Rajasthan State Bridge and Construction Corporation, Rajasthan State Seeds Corporation and Rajasthan State Cooperative Sheep and Wool Marketing Federation. In the period 1979-84, there has not been a significant change in the number of public enterprises. The three enterprises set up during this period are in the nature of promotional and development units. A feeling seems to have settled in the minds of policy makers that instead of adding to the number of the State Level Public Enterprises, it is useful to strengthen their working. New activities could be handed over to the existing enterprises.

Our study of the growth of State Level Public Enterprises shows that these enterprises have a wide spectrum of objectives ranging from exploitation of unexploited mineral development of industries in backward and tribal areas, provision of inputs for small industries, development of tourism to attract foreign exchange, housing for low-income people, provision of quick and efficient transport development of agriculture and dairy provision of power welfare of tribals and scheduled castes to the provision of marketing support to agriculturists and small scale industry, industrial promotion in the State through private and non-resident Indian entrepreneurs and revival of sick units.

The data on investment in State Level Public Enterprises are not available plan period-wise. According to a study by Sisodia the investment in statutory corporations and Government companies was of the order of Rs. 95.43 lakhs in 1963-64. This shot up to Rs. 179.81 lakhs in 1966-67. The 1980's have seen a gigantic increase in the investment in State Level Public Enterprises. During the years 1980-81, 1981-82, 1982-83 and 1984-85 the State Government investment in the State Level Public Enterprises in the form of share capital and term loans was of order of Rs. 571.91 crores, Rs. 608.91 crores, Rs. 670.10 crores, Rs. 745.59 crores and Rs. 814.11 crores, respectively. The total investment including the investment from State Government, Central Government and other sources was Rs. 919.74 crores in 1980-81, Rs. 1081.44, Rs. 1081.44 crores in 1981-82, Rs. 1252.89 crores in 1982-83,

Rs. 1425.52 crores in 1983-84 and Rs. 1588.16 crores in 1984-85.

The State Level Public Enterprises (SLPEs) have been organised into four forms, viz., Statutory Corporations/Boards, registered Government companies, Co-operative societies and Departmental undertakings. Of the 36 SLPEs as on 31st March 1985, seven were statutory corporations, 12 were Government companies, 13 were cooperative societies and four were departmental under- takings. The Statutory Corporations/ Boards have been set up for two reasons: (i) there have been central legislations with regard to the setting up of enterprise in the field of electricity, road transport, warehousing and provision of finance to the small enterpreneurs and the State Government prepared to take advantage of them, and (ii) the construction of houses on a very large scale for the people in the middle and lower income groups and weaker sections of society, land levelling and realienating of land and water courses as a part of command area development in the Chembal and Rajasthan Canal areas, as activities required greater freedom and a clear-cut framework of authority and control. The number of departmental undertakings has been static at four during the last 20 years. This is in line with the announcement made in the 1978 Industrial Policy of the Government of Rajasthan which proclaimed that for an efficient conduct of the State Level Public Enterprises, no departmental enterprises would be set up in the future. One of the reasons for the non-conversion of the departmental enterprises into Government Company or statutory corporations form has been that these enterprises are natural monopolies. However, the technology employed in their operations is very simple and has not under~one any marked change. The State Government set up in 1964 the Department of State Enterprises and placed the four departmental Enterprises--Rajasthan State Chemical Works, Sodium Sulphide Factory Didwana, and Rajasthan Government Salt Works, Didwana, and Rajasthan

Government Salt Works, Pachpadra under its direct control. This was done to overcome bottlenecks experienced by the departmental undertakings arising out of welfare amongst themselves and ensure the requisite coordination required from different departments in the Government for the problem-free working of these departmental undertakings. It is worth mentioning here that Rajasthan was the first State to set up a State Enterprises Department headed by a Senior officer from the Indian Administrative Service charged with the responsibility of managing the departmental undertakings and the units to be taken over from the Private sector. A peep into the evolution of the forms of organisation of Public Enterprises in India would reveal that this step was very similar to the creation of the Railway Board at the Centre to impart a greater operational and policy-making system and freedom to the Indian Railways. But later on, it was thought that it would be appropriate to set up State Level Public Enterprises in the form of Government companies to enable them to run on sound commercial lines. It was believed that the incorporation of Public Enterprises in the company form would allow an adequate measure of autonomy with regard to proper staffing and developing appropriate procedures, systems for purchasing, selling and financing business activities. Further, mobilisation of institutional finance also prompted the State Government to undertake certain economic activities in the form of Government companies. In an economically backward State like Rajasthan, where people's cooperation is a primary requirement for the success of any State programme, it was thought that activities such as dairying, sheep and wool marketing, tribal area development, shipping and Oilseeds processing needed to be supported in the State sector in the form of cooperative organisations. As this component of the public sector programme is substantial, the number of State Level Public Enterprises organised as cooperative societies is also very large.

Boards of Management

The Boards of the State Level Public Enterprises are both policy and functional types. But the majority of boards are of policy type. The boards in most of the cases do not have functional directors. Only the Rajasthan State Electricity Board and Rajasthan Housing Board have functional directors. The absence of the functional Director could be explained by the fact that the size of the State Level Public Enterprises in Rajasthan is small in terms of turnover and investment. The boards are heavily loaded with the official directors. A study of the boards reveals that on the whole. 62 per cent of the Board members are officials[2]. In the case of Rajasthan Small Industries Development Corporation there are as many as eight official members on the Board. There is no uniformity about the tenure of the board members. In the case of the statutory corporation excepting Rajasthan State Electricity Board the other enabling acts are silent on the tenure of the board members. In practice the tenure ranges from, maximum five years to the minimum of one year. The statutory corporations and the Government companies as per the provisions of the enabling Acts and the articles of association should have their board meetings at least once a month. However in practice the number of board meetings held varied from minimum of three to maximum of thirteen. The trend is in favour of having a non-official not holding an office of profit excepting in the case of the Rajasthan Small Industries Development Corporation as the Chairman. The Chairman-cum-Managing Director mode of appointing the head prevails in the Rajasthan State Electricity Board which is the biggest of State Level Public Enterprises in terms of both the turnover and investment. The professionals are not favoured as Chairman and Managing Directors of the State Level Public Enterprises. The representation of different groups on a board is missing. It is worth mentioning that the philosophy of workers' participation in management at the

Board level though accepted in the Industrial Policy Resolution of the Rajasthan Government in 1978 has not found favour with the State Level Public Enterprises. A study of the business done by the boards points out that a lot of time in the board meetings is devoted to the discussion of operational matters including transfers creating of new posts, Reinstatement of employees. This is natural in view of the fact that official directors on the boards superimpose the governmental views on different aspects of policy-making which as a matter of fact, should come under their domain.

Accountability

The accountability mechanisms in the State Level Public Enterprises are in no way different from those applicable to the Central Public Enterprises. Our study of the accountability problems reveals a striking similarity between the problems faced by the two sets of public enterprises. In the study on Public Accountability of Public Enterprises in Rajasthan, it was revealed that the question method of legislative control has been most popular in the case of State Level Public Enterprises in Rajasthan. However, most of the questions asked relate to the Rajasthan Road Transport Corporation and Rajasthan State Electricity Board. As per the study, the average questions asked per day were 30 in the fourth and fifth State Assemblies. Of these questions, the average of questions on public enterprises was 1.14. Of the total number of questions asked only 58 percent were replied to. The findings of the study by and large, stand good even during the current times. Almost all the questions are highly local in character and deal with routine matters. There are hardly any questions on the policy matters or long-term planning.

A legislative Committee on State Level Public Enterprises was set up in the year 1968. The systems and procedures adopted by the Committee are akin to those followed by the Committee on Public Undertakings at the Centre between

1968-69 and 1978-79 the companies brought out 74 reports. A study on the working of the Committee reveals that it has curtailed the Autonomy of State Level Public Enterprise by encroaching into the operational and sub-policy matters. During the period 1977-80, the Committee made recommendations on 58 policy matters, 117 sub-policy matters and 91 operational matters. The Committee has a membership of 15 and the record of the attendance shows that the members abstained freely. The reports of the Committee are seldom discussed in detail by the State Legislative Assembly. About half of the recommendations have not been accepted by the Government.

Financial Performance

The financial performance of State Level Public Enterprises in India has been a cause of great concern to the policy-makers and planners. This concern was shared publicly by the Prime Minister in one of his meetings with the planners last year. When the country is faced with a severe resource crunch, everything should be done to mobilise money from public investment for the welfare of the masses. Over three-and a half decades of the planned era, the State Government have invested a large sum of money in these enterprises. But the returns from the investments have been either negative or not worth the name. The Rajasthan scenario does not present a contrast. The Bureau of Public Enterprises of the Government of Rajasthan in its document titled "Public Enterprise Profile 1984-85" has presented data with regard to the financial performance of 33 enterprises for the year 1984-85. The data for Rajasthan State Agriculture Marketing Board, Rajasthan Tribal Area Development Cooperative Federation and Sri Keshoraipatan Cooperative Sugar Mills have not been presented in the report, as the first one of these enterprises was under the Central Government management and in the case of the other two enterprises the accounts could not be finalised. It may also be noted that of the 33 enterprises, figures for 14 enterprises were taken on the basis of provisional accounts. In fact, in the case of 9 Public Enterprises accounts were in arrears for more than three years. This shows that the accounting system in the State Level Public Enterprises is in a great mess.

The salient features of performance of the State Level Public Enterprises are as follows:

(i) The financial performance of State Level Public Enterprises is in doldrums. The net loss incurred by the State Level Public Enterprise increased from Rs. 14.98 crores in 1980-81 to Rs. 85.82 crores in 1984-85. The profit after tax to net worth was -11.24% in 1980-81 and 119.11% in 1984-85.

(ii) The earnings before interest and taxes provided almost insignificant coverage for interest payments.

(iii) The turnover to capital employed ratio is very low. In 1980- 81, the turnover of capital employed was 24.63%. This ratio declined to 24.10% in 1984-85. In other words, per one rupee of capital employed the goods produced sold amounted to 0.26 paise. In the case of Central Public Enterprises, the turn-over to capital employed ratio is around 1.51. In the neighbouring State of Gujarat, the ratio is 0.6:1. In Public Enterprises in U.S.S.R, this ratio is 5:1 and in private enterprises in India the turnover to capital ratio is 3.5:1. This ratio reveals that heavy over-investments had taken place in the creation of fixed assets and working capital. Further, the growth rate of turnover is dismal in the State Level Public Enterprises. This is borne out by the fact that the growth rate of turnover was 15.64% in the case of Central Public Enterprises in 1984-85 and 9.7% in the case of the State Level Public Enterprises in Gujarat in 1983-84.

(iv) The accumulated losses have eroded the investments in State Level Public Enterprises. Whereas the capital investment increased from Rs. 958.51 crores in 1980-81 to Rs. 1496.92 crores in 1983-84, the net worth declined from Rs. 133.36 crores in 1980-81 to Rs. 71-80 crores in 1984-85. Out of 33 enterprises, whose financial performance has been reported, 18 enterprises have increased their net worth; five enterprises have their net worth varying between 50 to 100% of paid-up capital and the net worth of 6 enterprises is below 50% of their paid-up capital. In the case of 4 enterprises, viz., Rajasthan State Electricity Board, Rajasthan State Road Transport Corporation, Rajasthan State Tanneries, Rajasthan Cooperative Dairy Federation, the net worth was negative. The net worth was unascertainable in the case of Rajasthan State Electricity Board and Rajasthan Cooperative Dairy Federation.

(v) The proportion of debt-to-equity was very uneven and decidedly against the interests of the State Level Public Enterprises. This could be seen from Table-I which apparently hints at the neglect of introduction of adequate amount of risk capital in the capitalisation of the State Level Public Enterprises.

TABLE 5.1

Debt-Equity Ratio in the State Level Public Enterprises in Rajasthan

(Rupees in lakh)

	1980-81	*1981-82*	*1982-83*	*1983-84*	*1984-85*
Debt	82544.24	97371.15	112974.22	128174.83	142512.66
Equity	8659.89	10773.34	12315.44	14377.93	16303.86
Debt-Equity Ratio	9.53:1	9.4:1	9.17:1	8.91:1	8.74:1

Status of SLPEs in Rajasthan

The Status of SLPEs in Rajasthan is given in the following table:

TABLE 5.2

Status of SLPEs in Rajasthan

(Rs. in Crore)

Rajasthan Years Items	1998-99	1999-00	2000-01	2001-02	2002-03	2003-04
1. Total no. of SLPEs*	24	24	24	28	28	26
2. No. of Working SLPEs	17	17	17	20	20	19
3. No.of Non-Working SLPEs	7	7	7	8	8	7
(i) Under Liquidation	1	1	1	1	2	
(ii) Under Closure	--	--	--	--	--	--
(iii) Under Merger	--	--	--	--	--	--
(iv) Others	6	6	6	7	6	
4. Total Equity	2379.15	2371.09	2266.65	2267.73	2630.9	3365.64
5. Total Debt	7809.75	9204.72	8571.84	9044.17	8413.22	10699.19
6. Total Investment	10188.90	11575.82	10838.49	11311.9	11044.12	14064.83
7. No.of Profit making enterprises	11	18	13	9	11	8
8. No.of Loss making enterprises	11	6	11	10	11	6
9. Net Profit/Loss	82.44	335.25	71.03	-53.81	-41.65	1146.82
10. Accumulated Loss(-)/Profit	-270.6	-299.12	-254.21	-317.87	-315.38	270.60

Source: Reports of the Comptroller and Auditor General of India (Commercial), on Rajasthan for 1998-99 to 2003-04.

(vi) The losses incurred by the Rajasthan State Electricity Board, Rajasthan Land Development Corporation, Rajasthan Co- operative Spinning Mills Private Limited, Gulabpura, Rajasthan State Mines and Minerals Limited and Rajasthan State Seeds Corporation amounted to 95.75 per cent of the losses incurred by 17 units in 1984-85. During the period 1980-81 to 1984-85, about 90% of losses have come from 5 major undertakings. A significant point to be noted is that only two undertakings, viz., Rajasthan

State Electricity Board and Rajasthan State Road Transport Corporation accounted for 76.5%, 92.80% and 86.16% and 90% of the total losses incurred in 1980-81, 1981-82, 1982-83, 1983-84 and 1984-85 respectively.

(vii) The high costs of operations were the major bone of the State Level Public Enterprises. The direct costs were disproportionate, the indirect expenses were very high, the selling and administrative expenses were not commensurate with the increases in turnover. The inordinately high debt- equity ratio added fuel to the fire by adding the high, interest charges. In fact, one-third of the State Level Public Enterprises were making cash losses.

(viii) The State Level Public Enterprises were characterised by the absence of costing Internal audit, budgeting and budgetary control systems. They had a very meagre autonomy in the area of price fixation. The rules regarding the recruitment and promotion were the carbon copies of the Government Service Regulations. They could not punish an erring employee and reward a sincere worker. The inventory control production planning and control and designing systems were in a low key. No attempt was made to differentiate between selling and marketing in many State Level Public Enterprises.

Towards a New Framework for the Management of State Level Public Enterprises

The State Policy pertaining to the State Level Public Enterprises places great reliance on them for the future growth and development of the economy of Rajasthan. Despite chronic losses, the State investment in these enterprises is increasing year after year at a phenomenal rate. This shows the concern of the State towards the growth of task. They must turn the corner and give evidence that they are more that public entities and are capable of not only standing on their own feet but also contributing to the State Exchequer. The following measures may help the State Level Public Enterprises in the operation face-lift.

(i) *Formation of turn around strategies:* The suggestions for toning up the performance mostly relate to financial areas. In our study of the State Level Public Enterprises we have come to believe that such an approach cannot work as it enables the analyst to see the problem in a compartmentalised way and not in its totality. We, therefore, suggest that to help the State Level Public Enterprises in coming out of the woods a turn around strategy formulated for each and every enterprise separately would be the basis right step. This will require the management of these Public Enterprises to commission a team of experts which would go into all sorts of details pertaining to the undertaking to find out as to where things have gone wrong. This team thereafter should work out a future plan of action as an integrated whole aimed at enabling the enterprises to commence the viable operations and subsequently writing off the accumulated losses. In the case of State Level Public Enterprises in Rajasthan this approach appears to have a greater potential as one-third of the Public Enterprises are incurring cash losses and another one-third have not been able to keep their head above the water. Some enterprises have become chronic losers whereas the others behave like the Rain God making profits once in a spell of 4 to 5 years.

Distincting Out from the Government

(ii) *The State Level Public Enterprises, over a period of time, distance out from the Government.* This would enable them to get the requisite autonomy in price fixation, speeding up recoveries, hiring and dismissing of personnel and ironing out the imbalances in the capital structure. Though one-third of the State Level Public Enterprises are registered as Government companies, none has approached the capital market.[5] Jaipur has now a Stock~ Exchange and this should be taken advantage of. It is difficult to understand as to why the State Level Public Enterprises in Rajasthan have not gone in for public deposits whereas their counterparts in many states mobilised money through this source.

(iii) *The operations management in the State Level Public Enterprises is an untapped area.* Starting from effective men and materials management, improved shop-floor operations; better utilisation of capacities and inculcating professionalisation in marketing activities would go a long way in making the State Level Public Enterprises financially viable. The over-staffing, which has been a bane of State Tanneries and Ganganagar Sugar Mills, should be immediately curbed in the other undertakings, too.

(iv) *Project Management:* Procedural formalities in the State Level Public Enterprises have delayed the implementation of projects; hence, cost escalation distributing the ratio of return on investments. The time and cost overruns have been frequent in the case of the State Level Public Enterprises in Rajasthan. The case of Hanumangarh Cooperative Spinning Mills is a recent example. The dispute with cost escalation clause with civil contractors and supplies of ring frame from Tax-Maco delayed the project by two years. This added to the cost of the project by more than Rs. 50 lakhs.

(v) *Professionalisation:* The State Level Public Enterprises have been manned at the top by non-officials and IAS/Rajasthan Administrative Service officers. As noticed earlier, their stay in Public Enterprises has been very brief and they seem to have promoted the tourist culture in these enterprises. An IAS 'or and officer from the Rajasthan Administrative Service is not necessarily a successful manager. Formation of management pool, proper screening of potential managers should be immediately resorted to. Human resources development in the State Level Public Enterprises should get its due place. Each State Level Public Enterprise should develop its training plan based on its own needs and Corporate Plan. Appropriate performance appraisal systems should be introduced. The Boards of Public Enterprises should be a homogeneous group of 7-9 persons representing different interest groups, including professionals. The representation of officers on the Board should be restricted to a maximum of two persons.

(vi) *The ideal would be only one.* The Board Members should get a reasonable tenure. The offices of the Chairmen and Managing Directors could be combined.

(vii) *Government machinery:* The Government machinery for the control of Public Enterprises should be infused with fresh blood. The BPE and the State Enterprises Department should have a greater role and clarity. Similarly, the need for the Public Investment Cell and the Public Investment Board need also to be re-examined. Instead of having a multiplicity of the controlling institutions, it would be appropriate to have a single body entrusted with the responsibility of coordinating the work of Public Enterprises and performing the role of nodal agency as elaborated by the Capoor Committee Report on the State Level Public Enterprises.

(viii) *Workers' Involvement:* The workers participation at the Board level should receive an utmost attention. The success of any productivity and profit implementation scheme hinges largely on their cooperation. The workers representation should be secured not only at the Board Level but also at the middle, lower and shop floor levels. This would ensure a successful introduction and implementation of quality circles in these enterprises.

Conclusion

The State Level Public Enterprises in Rajasthan are a post-independence phenomena. During the last 31/2 decades both their number and investment have multiplied phenomenally. The objectives of the State Level Public Enterprises have ranged from regional development and provision of basic inputs to agriculturist and small artisans to the industrialisation of the economy and earning surpluses for the growth of the economy as a whole. The professionalisation of the management of these enterprises and making them stand on their own have been the two major planks of the State Policy with regard to the management of these enterprises. However, the management practices and the financial performance of these enterprises have run contrary to these expectations. During the Sixth Plan Period in all the years all the State Level Public Enterprises taken together incurred huge losses and as a result, their networth declined rapidly. The excessive external controls, the unsound internal management, the unhealthy management of operations were primarily responsible for the loss making by these enterprises. If the State Level Public Enterprises have to turn the corner, they should design and implement suitable turn-around strategies and the Government should help them in an efficient: discharge of their functions by distancing them out to a great extent.

REFERENCES

1. Sharma, G.D., *Working of State Enterprises in Rajasthan*. Sterling Publications Private limited. New Delhi. 1975 pp. 8-17.
2. Niwal, T.C., *Management of Public Enterprises*, Capital Publishing House, Delhi, 1982, pp. 40-70.
3. Batra, Satish K. *Legislative Control over Public Enterprises*, Printwell Publishers, Jaipur, 1985, pp. 71-119.
4. Bureau of Public Enterprises (State Enterprises) Department. Government of Rajasthan, *Public Enterprises Profile 1984-85*, Jaipur, 1986, pp. 1-11.
5. Hooja, B State Level Public Enterprises in Rajasthan, in Mishra, R.K. and Ravishanker, S. (ed), *Management of State Level Public Enterprises in India*, National Publishing House, Delhi, 1988 (Forthcoming).
6. Department of Perfonnel & Administrative Reforms (Government of India, New Delhi), Report of the standing group on Management of Public Enterprises in the State, (HKL Capoor Committee Report), 1979.

11

Development and Performance of State Level Public Enterprises of Tamil Nadu

*C. Ramachandran**

This paper traces the growth of SLPEs in Tamilnadu and their current performance. It analyses the reasons responsible for suboptimal performance of the SLPEs and presents a framework for their turnaround.

Almost everywhere the 20th century has been a period of active involvement and participation by Governments in all aspects of economic life. Even the most enthusiastic adherent of private enterprises to-day accepts that public interest has to be assured by Government intervention and that all economies need policing by government. Traditional capitalism with its belief in the invisible hand, taking care of everything survives today only as a historic relic of the past. The quantum of national income both produced and spent by Government is on the increase in almost all the countries. India became free when socialism had almost become part of the conventional wisdom. The leaders of India's fight for freedom were considerably influenced by Fabian thought and the spectacular

* Commissioner & Secretary to Government, Department of Finance, Government of Tamil Nadu.

achievements of Society planned economy. This influence is clearly reflected in our policies since independence. Apart from Government being in Business and Industry as a guiding and regulating force, the industrial Policy Resolution stipulates how and when Government should run industry.

Prior to independence, things were totally different. British Law and justice were firmly established in India and a fairly stable and impartial administration was also a British legacy. But the fact that Britain had become the workshop of the world and the first industrialised nation in the world only confirmed India's position as a supplier of raw materials. India was the land of poverty, famine, starvation and misery as well as füedal pomp, riches and glory. In keeping with this common environment in the country, in 1947 when we achieved independence, Tamil Nadu had hardly any industry except a few textile mills. Industrialisation was the first priority of the Government.

The first State Level Financial Corporation, The Madras Industrial Investment Corporation (now called; Tamil Nadu Industrial Investment Corporation) was incorporated and registered under the Companies' Act on 26.3.1949 and commenced operations from 1.9.1949. Though registered under the Companies' Act, it was defined as a Banking Company but was exempted from the provisions of the Banking Companies' Act. This gave the Tamil Nadu Industrial Investment Corporation considerable flexibility and its separate identity continues even alter the passing of the State Finance Corporations Act though it performs the functions of a State Finance Corporation. The TIIC triggered the development of the engineering and foundry industry which laid the foundation for the automobile industry in Tamil Nadu. The share capital of the TIIC has been subscribed by the Government of Tamil Nadu (60 per cent), IDBI (25 per cent) and Pondicherry (5 per cent) and the balance amount by Insurance Companies, Cooperative Societies, Investment Trusts, etc. The activities of the TIIC now extends to Pondicherry. The Corporation provides long and medium- term loans, to industrial concerns mainly for the purpose of acquiring fixed assets, underwriting the issue of shares or debentures and guarantee/counter-guarantees, deferred payments, payment contracts, etc. TIIC also grants foreign currency loans through World Bank credit. Starting from a modest Rs. 13.75 lakhs gross sanctions in 1949-50, the activities of the Corporation have grown to Rs. 7017 lakhs gross sanctions in 1986-87.

The other organisations in the field of industrial development are:

1. Industrial Development Corporation Ltd. (TIDCO)
2. State Industries Promotion Corporation of Tamil Nadu Ltd. (SIPCOT)
3. Small Industries Development Corporation Ltd. (SIDCO)
4. Small Industries Corporation Ltd. (TANSI)

TIDCO, a fully owned Government Company is engaged in and running large scale public sector units and in joint sector projects. The management of the joint units is left to the private promoters. TIDCO's is through a Board of Directors and Sub-Committees TIDCO contributes 26 per cent of the equity while the private promoter contributes 25 per cent. The first joint sector unit to be promoted was the SPIC., the present share value of which is an indication of the public confidence in this venture. Joint sector units promoted by TIDCO now produce fertilisers, chemicals, pharmaceuticals, T.V. sets, Cigarettes, Batters, Castings and Forgings, etc., State Industries Promotion Corporation of Tamil Nadu (SIPCOT) was set up in 1971 as a public limited company wholly owned by Government of Tamil Nadu with an authorised capital of Rs. 5 Crores. SIPCOT promotes and develops medium and major industries actively working towards industrial dispersal and the development of industrially backward areas.

SIPCOT provides the following assistance:

1. A package, incentive like:
   (a) subsidy for feasibility studies
   (b) interest free sales tax loan
   (c) subsidy on fixed assets
   (d) concessional power tariff for HT supply, and
   (e) concessional water royalties.
2. Development of infrastructure in potential growth centres in the backward areas of the State and provision of this infrastructure at economic cost on soft payment terms.
3. Provisions of finance to medium and major industries under the IDBI scheme for refinance, and
4. Provision of various ancillary services.

The Tamil Nadu Small Industries Development Corporation (SIDCO) was incorporated as a private limited company on 23.3.1970 and converted into a public limited company on 29.1.1971. This is engaged in the following activities:

1. Construction of purchase worksheds and selling these on hire
2. Supply of machinery under hire purchase
3. Procurement and distribution of essential raw materials
4. Marketing assistance to small scale industrial units
5. Disbursement of Central capital subsidy to SSI units in backward areas.

6. Import and promotion distribution of raw materials and export promotion
7. Management of industrial estates
8. Sanction of loan to small scale industries.

TANSI was formed in 1965 to take over a number of small industrial units started from the first three Plans and initially run as department undertakings by the Directorate of Industries. The product range was wide. They cover:

1. Structurals
2. Forged, pressed and pressure die cast components
3. Hospital equipment
4. Furniture
5. Agricultural implements
6. Trailers
7. C.I. pipes and specials
8. Enamelled wires
9. Machined components
10. Processed hair
11. Finished leather
12. Footwear and leather products
13. Cycles
14. Mopeds
15. Machine tools.

Agriculture: In the agricultural sector there are 6 Corporations operating in Tamil Nadu:

1. Tamil Nadu Agro Industries Corporation
2. Tamil Nadu Sugarcane Farm Corporation
3. Tamil Nadu Forest Plantation Corporation

4. Tamil Nadu Tea Plantation Corporation
5. Tamil Nadu Medical Plant Farms Corporation
6. Arasu Rubber Corporation

Tamil Nadu Agro Industries Corporation Ltd.

This was incorporated in July 1966 with a view to encourage the growth and modernisation of agriculture, animal husbandry, food processing, etc. Presently, the main activities of the Corporation are purchase and sale of tractors, power tillers, implements and spares, production and sale of pesticides, nylon and polythene webbings and oil products, etc. The Corporation is also engaged in the sale of fertilizers on behalf of SPIC on an agency basis.

Tamil Nadu Sugarcane Farm Corporation

This Corporation was formed on 22.2.1972 at Vadapathimangalam in Thanjavur district to manage the surplus lands taken over under the Land Ceiling Act from Thiru Aruran Sugars Limited, Vadapathimangalam. It was started with a total area of 6528 acres of land under its control. Out of this, an extent of 2476.26 acres constituted lease lands which were released in 1980-81. The balance 4051.74 acres are now under its control. Out of this, 3682.57 acres are cultivable lands and the balance 369.17 acres are not fit for cultivation due to low level and poor drainage conditions. The Corporation is mainly concentrating on the cultivation of paddy and sugarcane. Due to lack of irrigation facilities and increased cost of cultivation, the Corporation has been suffering losses ever since its inception and the Government are considering its winding up.

Tamil Nadu Forest Plantation Corporation

This Corporation was started mainly to raise forest plantations of eucalyptus hybrid, cashew and cashewnut in the Government lands taken over on lease basis for industrial purposes and also to meet the demands for fuel and other forest produce in Tiruchirapalli, Pudukottai, Karaikudi and Vridchalam areas. The Corporation has now widened its activities and it is engaged in the manufacture of spirit and non-spirit based products, such as picture varnish, thinner, scaling wax, honey, etc.

Tamil Nadu Tea Plantation Corporation (TANTEA)

TANTEA was registered in 1975 as a Corporation with its head quarters in Coonoor in order to rehabilitate repatriates from Sri Lanka by raising tea plantations in the Government forest lands in the Nilgiris district. The Government took over a total of 1517.56 hectares of forest lands. Their lands were transferred to the Corporation on lease, the lease amount being fixed by Government from time to time. According to the project report, the Corporation was to bring under its purview a total area of 2240 hectares within a period of 30 years. The Corporation was able to achieve this within 8 years.

Tamil Nadu Medicinal Plant Farms Corporation

The TAMPCOL was established in September 1983 with the main objective of producing and selling herbal products, procurement and sale of raw materials used in Indian medicines and other herbal supplies and for developing Medicinal Plant Farms in Tamil Nadu. The present activities of the Corporation are the production of herbal hair tonic and crude drugs.

Arasu Rubber Corporation

Government of Tamil Nadu formed a separate Corporation by name Arasu Rubber Corporation Limited in August 1984 to take over the existing commercial and developmental activities of the Forest Department in respect of rubber plantation in the district of Kanyakumari and develop the existing plantations besides planting new areas and also to manage the factories processing rubber. The Corporation actually commenced business with effect from 1st October 1984.

Transport

Transport plays a vital role in development and the nationalisation of transport services has been the accepted policy since independence. In Tamil Nadu in 1947, 30 Government buses were introduced into the Madras City Transport System and in 1948, Madras City Transport was nationalised. The system initially functioned as a Government department. In 1959, it was decided to run express buses in all exceeding 120 Km. in length and in 1967-68, it was decided to nationalise (i) all routes exceeding 75 miles (ii) all routes from or terminating in Madras City, and (iii) all routes in Kanyakumari district.

In 1971, passenger transport services in the State were nationalised and Transport Corporations were formed as separate corporate entities under the Companies' Act 1956. The has been to have separate Corporation of optimum size and the Company ;form of organisation given flexibility and The financial working of the Transport units was considerably helped by the formation of Transport Development Limited (TDFC). In July 1975, Reserve Bank of India accepted this Company as a hire purchase finance Company.

Tamil Nadu Civil Supplies Corporation Limited

A sound public distribution is a prerequisite developing economy. The Tamil Nadu Civil Supplies Corporation which was incorporated on 24.7.1972 under the Companies' Act fulfills this role. It commenced business from 1.7.72 starting with a modest sales turnover of less than Rs. 12 crores and 1985-86, the turnover was Rs. 580 crores. In the first year its operation in 1973-74, the Corporation took over, in a phased manner fro the Civil Supplies Department the closing stocks rice, sugar and wheat in 13 godowns and in all the retail shops. It took over from the Civil Supplies Department responsibility for distribution of rice in the committed consisting of Madras City, Coimbatore and Kanyakumari. It undertook distribution of sugar, wheat and wheat products specified areas allotted by the Commissioner of Civil Supplies. The Corporation made a beginning in the field of procurement of paddy and rice from 1973 itself through levy and direct purchase. It also took over from the Co-operative management and control of 13 sick modern rice mills. The scarcity conditions then prevailing and to stabilise prices, the Corporation undertook procurement of pulses from the States for distribution in Tamil Nadu. In addition to running retail shops taken overt the Corporation opened 25 retail shops. During its second year of operation (1973-74) Corporation was made the sole nominee of the Government not, for the procurement and distribution of rice but also handling the entire quantities of sugar, wheat and wheat products allotted to the State. The Corporation established 38 purchase centres during the Samba 1974 season for procurement paddy. Besides meeting local demand of the public distribution system, the Corporation also sold paddy/rice to the States Gujarat, Karnataka, Kerala, Maharashtra and West Bengal.

Food situation in 1974-75 was very difficult and the Supplies Corporation rose to the occasion. In June 1974, market price of rice went upto Rs. 7 per Kg. and the strain on the public distribution system was great. Adhoc distribution rice was commenced from August 1974 and the local paddy and rice was intensified by operation 361 direct purchase centres. The entire movement of paddy was handled by the Corporation without associating any hullin agents. Even in 1974, the Corporation opened more fair price shops and started selling of essential commodities on a no profit no loss basis. The edible oils, chillies, pulses, soaps and other essentials were made available at reasonable prices. In September 1974, it was decided to eliminate all private dealers in the distribution of Government stocks and their place was taken by shops run by TNCSE or Cooperatives.

Due to procurement of heavy quantities of paddy/rice and holding them in stock for considerable periods, the corporation incurred heavy expenditure by way of interest, storage charges and storage losses. The Corporation had, therefore, to approach the State Government for the first time during 1978-79 for subsidy to cover buffer stock operation.

In July 1982, the Chief Minister's Nutritious Noon Meal Scheme was launched by Government and it is the Corporation which supplies rice, dal and edible oil to 65,000 noon meal centres spread over the State. The success of the scheme owes in no small measure to the organisational build up of the Civil Supplies Corporation. The Corporation has also been entrusted with some other special schemes like supply of essential commodities to Police personnel, rice to poor widows, the handicapped and the old age pensioners and tooth powder to the children fed in the noon meal centres.

Control Systems in State Public Sector Enterprises

These Public Sector Enterprises have internal as well as external control systems. Internal control is exercised through its Board of Directors as per the provision of Companies' Act, Articles of Association, and by the special acts by which they were formed. The external control is through the administrative departments in Secretariat. Legislature, Committee on Public Undertakings, State Bureau of Public Enterprises and the C & AG. The control through external agencies are briefly described below:

The Public Sector Enterprises of the State are controlled directly by the Administration incharge of the Corporation. The Articles of Association of the State Enterprises, which are wholly owned by the Government provide a clause empowering the Government to issue directive or call for such information as they deem necessary and the enterprises have to comply with such directives or furnish such information as are called for by the Government. The Government of Tamil Nadu have the power to-

1. give directions to the corporations in the exercise performance of their day-to-day functions;
2. call for such returns, accounts and other information as may be required from time to time;
3. approve the Corporation's annual budget estimates and project reports.

The Administrative Ministry has issued directives regarding the policy to be adopted in the matter of recruitment priorities to be given to Scheduled Castes and Scheduled Tribes and other category of people in recruitment, provision of labour welfare measures, housing facilities etc. The Administrative Ministry also controls the Government Companies in respect of creation of certain categories of posts, appointment of managerial personnel, fixing their remuneration etc. The Articles of Association of Government Companies provide that approval of the Government shall be obtained in respect of proposals regarding capital expenditure, increasing or reducing the authorised capital, winding up of the company, alteration of Memorandum or Articles of Association of the Company, etc.

The Administrative departments call for a number of returns, quarterly performance reports, resources statements, etc., from the Corporation under the control by way of monitoring their performance. The annual budget estimates of the corporations are obtained by the administrative departments for scrutiny and approval. The capital and revenue budgets are examined in consultation with Finance Department. Follow up action is also pursued wherever lapses are pointed out for purpose of rectification. While approving the budget main focus is on the allocation of resources to various schemes and it is ensured that the financial provision made by the Corporations in their budget is in line with the provisions made by the Government in their budget.

Legislature Control

Legislature control is a peculiar feature of Government companies arising out of accountability of the Executive to the State Legislature. Legislature exercises control through the mechanism of seeking information through questions on the working of the Government Companies. The copies of annual accounts of the Government Companies are laid on the table of the Legislature on which also discussions are held by the Members of the State Legislature. Control is also effected through its various committees of which the committee on Public Undertakings (COPU) plays an effective role in monitoring the performance of the State Undertakings.

Committee on Public Undertakings (COPU)

The question of setting up of a Parliamentary Committee on Public Undertakings was first discussed in the Lok Sabha in 1953 and the creation of a separate Parliamentary Committee to look into the affairs of the various categories of Public Corporations, Companies and Institutions was suggested but it was not accepted by the Government. Only in 1963, it was constituted and the Committee for Tamil Nadu was constituted in April 1973.

The COPU consists of 16 members elected by the Assembly from amongst their members according to the principle of proportionate representation by means of single transferable vote. The Chairman of the Committee on Estimates is an Ex-officio Member of the COPU. The Chairman of the Committee is appointed by the Speaker from amongst the members of the Committee. In his absence, one of the members elected by the Committee presides. The term of the Committee is one year.

The Committee examines the reports and accounts of the undertakings which have been specifically allotted to it and the reports of the Comptroller and Auditor General of India on these undertakings and ascertain whether the affairs of the undertakings are being managed in accordance with sound business principles and prudent commercial practices having regard to autonomy and efficiency of the management. The Committees also consider what economies and improvement in organisational efficiency or administrative reform consistent with general policy of the undertaking can be effected. In short. the function of the committee is generally to evaluate the performance of the under- takings covering all aspects like implementation of policies, programmes management, financial working etc.

State Bureau of Public Enterprises

With the growth in the number of Government Companies. the need for uniform set of rules and policies has become highly imperative. The State Bureau of Public Enterprises was set up in the Finance Department in January 1982 as a nodal agency to integrate and strengthen the arrangements for coordination and monitoring of all aspects of the management of Public Enterprises covering technical, economic, financial and managerial policy areas. The Bureau of Public Enterprises acts as an important agency for appraising investments in Public Enterprises. The performance of the Public Enterprises is reviewed by a Committee of Secretaries on Public Enterprises and the Bureau of Public Enterprises acts as the Secretariat to the Committee.

The advisory, monitoring and consultancy role of the Bureau of Public Enterprises may be summarised as follows:

1. To act as a Secretariat to the Committee of Secretaries

for convening the meetings, preparation of agenda, recording the minutes of the Meeting and taking follow up action.

2. To provide assistance to the concerned administrative departments in making a thorough expert and comprehensive scrutiny and evaluation of detailed Project reports and feasibility studies of new investment proposals and in particular assist the Department of Finance in this regard.

3. To collect, analyse, collate and monitor data based on audited and provisional figures of financial performance and prepare Annual Review on the performance of Public Sector Undertakings, prepare and furnish periodical reports on 20 point Programme to Government of India through the Planning and Development Department of the State. In addition, BPE undertakes in-depth studies of Public Sector Enterprises identified for the purpose so as to assist the concerned department in improving the managerial performance efficiency of these enterprises.

4. To undertake cost studies so as to assist the concerned department in taking decisions on pricing of certain raw materials

5. To collect and collate data from Public Sector Undertakings and furnish report to COPU by way of answering its remarks in the course of its examination of audit comments of C & AG relating to various Public Sector Undertakings of Tamil Nadu.

6. To compile and analyse information on service conditions of employees in Public Sector and to advise Government with a view to ensuring rationalisation where possible and bring about desirable uniformity in these matters as well as to advise and assist on wages and salary policy and other related matters.

7. To advise on matters regarding the procedural aspects in the formation of new corporation and to scrutinise the Memorandum and Articles of Association of the newly formed Corporations.
8. To scrutinise the Agenda of the Board Meetings of the Government Companies/Boards and assist the Finance Directors in this regard.
9. To advise and assist the concerned department on matters in which advice and assistance are sought.
10. To assist as a data bank and as a clearing house information in respect of important matters relating Public Sector Undertakings.

Comptroller and Auditor General of India

Accountability of the Government Companies to the Citizens through Legislature is secured through regulatory audit conducted by professional auditors. However, due to its inadequacy, C & AG plays an important role and assists the legislature in reviewing the performance of the Government Company. This audit conducted by the C & AG is propriety audit. The propriety audit is a continuous one. The audit points are raised whenever areas of weakness and extravagance are located. These audit points are routed through ,the administrative department of the Government Company. The comments of the Government Companies are referred to the Committee on Public Undertakings. The Committee calls upon the concerned Administrative Department to furnish such information as it requires.

Internal Management System

1. Composition of Board of Directors Including Chairman

The Chairman of a Government Company is appointed either on full time basis or on part-time basis, depending on the need of the Corporation, generally from among Civil servants though of late non-officials are appointed in increasing number. In the case of Statutory Boards, non-officials are appointed as Chairman. Similarly, in the case of Managing Directors, almost all the undertakings are managed by full time Managing Directors except a few which are managed by part-time Managing Directors who are normally the Heads of Department concerned. Most of the Managing Directors are appointed from IAS cadre officers. In some cases, technically qualified persons are also appointed as Managing Directors, where the need for the technical expertise is felt. For instance, all the passenger transport undertakings are managed by Engineers. Similar is the case with State Construction Corporation Limited; an Engineer is holding the post of Managing Director.

The Board generally consists of the following addition to the Managing Director:

1. One senior official in the rank of Deputy Secretary or above from Finance Department as Finance Director.
2. One representative of the concerned Administrative Department who is also in the rank of Deputy Secretary or above.
3. One representative of the Head of the Department concerned.
4. One Technical Director.

Some eminent enterpreneurs with practical background and business experience are also appointed as non-official Directors and Chairmen.

The Board of Directors is given unfettered powers by the Articles of Association in all matters except some financial and recruitment powers like the following in respect of which prior approval of the Government has to be obtained.

(i) Capital expenditure exceeding Rs. 10 lakhs at a time.

(This limit will not apply to operators of financial institutions)

(ii) For creation of any post in the State Public Sector Undertaking, if the maximum of time scale of pay for the post is Rs. 4050/- per month or more and for appointment of any person in any post if the maximum of time scale of pay for the post is Rs. 3090/- per month or more.

All the State Public Sector Undertakings were directed to prepare budgets incorporating the corporate objectives, targets for that year and should plan its expenses in such a way that there should not be wide variations in the plan and performance. The Government have also directed that these Corporations should have internal control through internal audit conducted by qualified Chartered/Cost .Accountants. The other internal management systems like MIS are being introduced in these undertakings gradually and it may take some more time before all the State Public Sector Undertakings in this State are having adequate and full-fledged internal control systems envisaged.

Policies regarding production, marketing, personnel, finance and general management are as decided by the Board of Directors of the respective Corporation. State Government does not interfere in these matters.

These Corporations are being managed strictly in accordance with the provision of Companies' Act. They have the flexibility and autonomy in conducting their internal management and Government does not interfere with their day-to-day functions. Composition of their Board, tenure, emoluments, frequency of board meeting are as per the regulations contained in their Articles of Association and subject to the provisions of the Companies Act.

The human resource management of these undertakings are also handled by their Boards subject to certain broad guide-line from Government. All the Public Sector Undertakings should get the prior approval of State Government for making appointment of personnel to a post and creation of a post, the maximum scale of pay of which is Rs. 3050/- per month and Rs. 4050/- per month respectively and for all other cases, the management is competent to do the spade work.

Investment Decision

State Public Sector Undertakings have to get the approval of State Government for making capital investment exceeding Rs. 10 lakhs and all the projects promoted by these undertākings are required to be approved by Government after placing the matter before its board.

Total Performance

As on 31.3.1986, there were 74 Government Companies (including 1 subsidiary). The aggregate paid up capital as on 31.3.1986 stood at Rs. 301.45 crores. Out of these, 13 companies engaged in passenger transport (with an investment of Rs. 29.75 crores) and 5 companies with an investment of Rs. 41.22 crores are undertaking financing work wholly or partly.

The balance of long term loans outstanding in respect of 32 as on 31.3.86 was Rs. 569.85 crores. The above figures include (a) outstanding loans of Rs. 136.66 crores from 13 companies engaged in passenger transport and (b) outstanding loans of Rs. 296.95 crores from 4 companies engaged in financing or partly.

State Government guaranteed repayment of loans raised by 22 companies and payment of interest thereon. The amounts guaranteed and loans outstanding against this as on 31.3.1986 were 376.30 and Rs. 266.09 crores respectively. The gross turnover 1985-86 reached an impressive growth of about Rs.

1680 as against Rs. 1283 crores in 1984-85. The Tamil Nadu Civil Supplies Corporation and the Passenger Transport Corporations have contributed about 79 percent of the turnover during 1985-86. Passenger Transport Corporations alone employ about 74,561 persons against the total figure of 1,28,310.

As regards the working results of the important companies, the picture is given in Table 11.1 and 11.2.

TABLE 11.1

Detail of Profit Earned/Loss Suffered by State Public Undertaking During 1981-82 to 1985-86 Net Profit (+)/Loss (-) (Rupees in Lakhs)

Sl. No.	*Name of the Corporation*	*1981-82*	*1982-83*	*1983-84*	*1984-85*	*1985-86*
1	Anna Transport Corporation	(-) 65.63	(+) 37.04	(+) 37.16	(+) 29.22	(+) 2.84
2	Cheran Transport Corporation	(+) 9.39	(+) 18.80	(+) 62.32	(+) 54.13	(-) 9.14
3	Cholan Roadways Corporation	(-) 168.10	(+) 60.67	(-) 26.62	(+) 119.69	(+) 15.35
4	Dheeran Chinnamalai Transport Corporation	--	--	--	--	(+) 7.06
5	Jeeva Transport Corporation	--	--	(+) 1.55	(+) 1.27	(+) 0.23
6	Kattabomman Transport Corporation	(-) 32.32	(+) 60.96	(-) 19.39	(-) 4.03	(+) 2.49
7	Marudhu Pandiar Transport Corporation	--	--	(+) 0.48	(+) 0.74	(+) 0.80
8	Nesamony Transport Corporation	--	--	(+) 0.76	(+) 0.16	(+) 4.78
9	Pandyan Roadways Corporation	(-) 28.60	(-) 22.61	(-) 27.20	(+) 24.82	(+) 46.43
10	Pallavan Transport Corporation	(-) 913.01	(-) 778.51	(-) 1002.68	(-) 715.23	(+) 54.10
11	Pattukottai Azhagiri Transport Corporation	(-) 266.02	(-) 134.96	(-) 196.08	(+) 17.36	(+) 60.00
12	Thanthai Periyar Transport Corporation	(-) 141.21	(+) 47.53	(+) 103.42	(+) 143.20	(+) 39.21
13	Thiruvalluvar Transport Corporation	(-) 259.53	(-) 82.68	(+) 57.79	(+) 36.85	(-) 60.77
14	Tamil Nadu Goods Transport Corporation	(-) 16.75	(+) 0.33	(+) 11.40	(+) 9.15	(+) 3.63

Sl. No.	Name of the Corporation	1981-82	1982-83	1983-84	1984-85	1985-86
15	Poompuhar Shipping Corporation	(+) 31.87	(+) 33.55	(+) 19.43	(+) 34.06	(+) 155.17
16	Anna Engineering Corporation	(+) 0.89	(+) 0.28	(+) 0.25	(+) 0.50	(+) 0.54
17	Charan Engineering Corporation	(+) 0.55	(+) 2.90	(-) 2.00	(+) 1.00	--
18	Cholan Engineering Corporation	(-) 1.73	(-) 0.30	--	--	--
19	Madurai Pandian Engineering Corporation	(+) 3.14	(+) 0.93	(+) 0.52	(-) 2.95	(-) 4.60
20	Pallavan Engineering Corporation	--	--	--	--	--
21	Tamil Nadu Small Industries Corporation	(-) 106.26	(-) 183.59	(-) 211.30	(-) 443.35	(-) 420.46
22	Southern Structurals Limited	(-) 201.73	(-) 201.53	(+) 110.76	(+) 43.96	(+) 44.90
23	Tamil Nadu Zari Limited	(-) 0.08	(+) 3.45	(+) 7.17	(-) 0.16	(+) 2.62
24	Tamil Nadu Ceramics Limited	(-) 11.54	(-) 20.60	(-) 49.92	(-) 62.66	(-) 84.21
25	Tamil Nadu Sugar Corporation	(+) 150.57	(+) 15.70	(-) 38.45	(-) 112.17	(+) 169.90
26	Tamil Nadu Salt Corporation	(-) 24.50	(-) 44.58	(-) 44.58	(-) 39.58	(-) 30.10
27	Electronics Corporation of Tamil Nadu	(-) 2.83	(-) 41.19	(-) 68.91	(-) 59.74	(-) 56.96
28	Tamil Nadu News Print and Papers Ltd.	--	--	--	-	(-) 2034.29
29	Tamil Nadu Magnesite Ltd.	(+) 18.25	(+) 11.99	(+) 10.31	(+) 1.46	(-) 61.67
30	Tamil Nadu Minerals Ltd.	9.50	(+) 11.04	(+) 28.42	(+) 34.83	(+) 41.86
31	Tamil Nadu Civil Supplies Corporation	(-) 2888.82	(-) 5649.16	(-) 5266.27	(-)10996.33	(-) 15653.88
32	Tamil Nadu State Marketing Corporation	--	--	(-)62.00	(+) 1.00	(+) 8.00
33	Tamil Nadu Small Industries Corporation	(+) 0.37	(+) 10.89	(+) 16.29	(+) 44.01	(+) 18.63
34	Tamil Nadu Industrial Investment Corporation	(+) 0.37	(+) 10.89	(+) 16.29	(+) 44.01	(+) 18.63
35	State Industries Promotion Corporation	(+) 53.37	(+) 59.91	(+) 70.42	(+) 63.06	(+) 142.81
36	Tamil Nadu Industrial Development Corporation	(+) 166.54	(+) 204.51	(+) 163.03	(+) 207.80	(+) 15.45

Sl. No.	*Name of the Corporation*	*1981-82*	*1982-83*	*1983-84*	*1984-85*	*1985-86*
37	Tamil Nadu Transport Development Finance Corporation	(+) 4.93	(+) 3.78	(+) 3.60	(+) 4.24	(+) 4.45
38	Tamil Nadu Handloom Development Corporation	(+) 5.84	(-) 0.27	(+) 5.84	(+) 2.60	(+) 3.63
39	Tamil Nadu Textile Corporation	(+) 3.18	(-) 20.12	(-) 1.33	(-) 1.63	(-) 26.09
40	Tamil Nadu Theatre Corporation	(+) 0.22	(+) 2.24	(-) 1.33	(-) 1.63	(+) 1.33
41	Tamil Nadu Tourism Development Corporation	(-) 0.07	(+) 7.26	(+) 17.05	(+) 1.73	(-) 0.83
42	Tamil Nadu Handicrafts Development Corporation	(+) 9.52	(+) 3.94	(+) 2.34	(-) 3.09	(+) 7.88
43	Tamil Nadu Poultry Development Corporation	(-) 33.75	(-) 3.88	(-) 1.19	(-)4.79	(+) 13.81
44	Tamil Nadu Fisheries Development Corporation	(-) 128.03	(-) 126.05	(+) 16.45	(+) 22.80	(-) 23.96
45	Dharmapuri District Development Corporation	(+) 2.14	(+) 2.06	(+) 0.66	(+) 4.05	(+) 2.41
46	Tamil Nadu Backward Classes Economic Development Corporation	--	(-) 3.69	(-) 7.29	(-) 7.71	(-) 7.90
47	Tamil Nadu Leather Development Corporation	--	--	(-) 2.06	(-) 4.85	(-) 9.22
48	Tamil Nadu Corporation for Development Women Ltd.	--	--	--	(+) 0.15	(+) 0.93
49	Tamil Nadu Agro Industries Corporation	(+) 1.37	(-) 41.20	(-) 33.63	(-) 30.41	(+) 4.96
50	Tamil Nadu Sugarcane Farms Corporation	(-) 12.28	(-) 14.28	(-) 24.89	(-) 42.40	(-) 35.36
51	Tamil Nadu Forest Plantation Corporation	(-) 50.97	(-) 2.32	(+) 21.83	(-) 49.45	(+) 45.96
52	Tamil Nadu Tea Plantation Corporation	(-) 58.30	(+) 7.62	(+) 163.11	(+) 121.10	(+) 119.75
53	Tamil Nadu Medical Plant and Herbal Medicinal Corporation Ltd.	--	--	(-) 0.31	(-) 0.06	(+) 0.47
54	Arasu Rubber Corporation	--	--	--	(+) 1.95	(+) 11.55
55	Tamil Nadu Addravidar Housing and Development Corporation	(-) 40.99	(-) 29.77	(-) 20.85	(-) 40.05	(+) 19.53
56	Tamil Nadu State Construction Corporation	(-) 5.99	(-) 17.19	(-) 76.81	(+) 3.80	(+) 34.29

Sl. No.	*Name of the Corporation*	*1981-82*	*1982-83*	*1983-84*	*1984-85*	*1985-86*
57	Tamil Nadu Police Housing Corporation	(-) 5.69	(-) 14.82	(-) 23.00	(-) 4.14	(+) 6.79
58	Tamil Nadu State Tubewell Corporation	-	(-) 16.56	(-) 24.97	(-) 23.03	(-) 20.50
59	Tamil Nadu Warehousing Corporation	(+) 65.71	(+) 79.65	(+) 95.17	(+) 119.23	(+) 183.15
60	Overseas Manpower Corporation	(-) 2.06	(-) 2.60	(-) 3.83	(-) 2.80	(+) 7.29
61	Tamil Nadu Meat Corporation	(-) 2.76	(-) 2.35	(-) 2.73	(-) 6.94	(-) 9.24
62	Tamil Nadu Chit Corporation	--	--	--	--	--
63	Pallavan Transport Consultancy Services	--	--	--	(+) 0.01	(+) 0.57

TABLE 11.2

(Rupees in lakhs)

Investment (as on 31.3.86)	*State Govt.*	*Others*
Share Capital	26778.28	5202.05
Share Advance	2525.69	--
Total	29303.97	5202.05
Long Term Loan		
Total Investment	12191.20	68044.40
	41495.17	73246.45

Forty companies finalised their accounts and of these, 27 companies including 4 subsidiaries earned profits aggregating 8.19 crores and 13 companies incurred losses aggregating Rs. 8.08 crores during the year 1985-86.

As is apparent from the previous paragraph, the investment in the public sector has not produced adequate finance benefits. In the public sector, a company is promoted only if promoters are sure that the organisation can at least sustain itself. The same principle must be followed by the public sector at least in cases where it is adopting the company form organisation.

Very often, a company is registered (i) to avail institutional finance and to avoid departmental regulations and procedures. Thus, functions which are normally discharged by Government departments and in some cases continue to be mainly handled by the departments, are simultaneously handed over partially to a newly registered Government company. The share capital is used to meet the establishment expenditure and soon the accumulated losses exceed the initial investment. It has to be made mandatory that at least in cases where it uses a company form of organisation, it should stand on its own legs and depend on Government budgetary support for day to day operatic One way of achieving this would be to insist that the Government Companies should raise at least a sizable portion of their equity by public subscription, to the share capital. If combersome procedures are preventing Government departments from achieving results, the remedy lies in changing the procedures and not handing over part of its functions to the newly formed companies. In theory, success should not be confined to the partial area allotted to the company and if a department's failure to achieve expected results is due to its adherence to procedures, what is called for is change in departmental procedures.

In practice, it is not merely the financial results but (the physical results which are poorer in the newly formed Com) than in the Government department. A quick look of all Government Companies is necessary and where they have been following by carving out a part of the functions a Government department the Company should be wound up and its functions are handed 1 to the department concerned in cases where the financial results do not justify the Company's continuance.

A case study where such action was taken by the of Tamil Nadu is narrated below:

The Tamil Nadu State Farms Corporation

The TNSFC was set up on 5th December 1974 with the objective of increasing agricultural production in Tamil Nadu by taking up cultivation of loans which were lying waste. It was estimated that approximately 11.00 lakh acres were lying waste under the classification "Cultivable Waste". These lands were owned by the Government of Tamil Nadu and had not been formed, or put to other use. because of the severe limitations that existed such as rockiness, frequent droughts. total lack of possibilities for flow-irrigation from river systems, salinity, water logging. excessive weed growth etc. The SFC was formed to take these lands on lease and start active cultivation.after necessary reclamation. The lease was fixed for 35 years at the rate of Rs. 50 per acre per year. The lands were divided into farm units of 250 acres each, which were under the supervision of a Deputy Farm Superintendent in the cadre of Deputy Agriculture Officer and groups of such units were placed under the supervision of a Chief Farm Superintendent in the cadre of a District Agricultural Officer. The farms raised paddy, groundnut, cotton, sugarcane, banana etc. under irrigated conditions. Water for irrigation was made available by sinking deep tubewells for which the Corporation had acquired 6 drilling rigs. In order to expedite waste prospecting, the Corporation had hired additional rigs from the Department of Agriculture and the TWAD also.

The Corporation started with an authorised share capital of one crore of 10,000 shares of 1,000 each. The equity capital of the Corporation was contributed both by the State Government and the Central Government. The Government of India provided equity as the Ceylon repatriates were being rehabilitated by the Corporation. The Corporation accommodated 1300 Ceylon repatriate candidates as Agricultural labourers on its farms. In the first year, operation in 1975-76 the Corporation took over two existing farms viz.,

TABLE 11.3

(Rupees in lakhs)

Investment (as on 31.3.86)	*State Govt.*	*Others*
Investment in State Transport Undertakings (as on 31.3.86)		
Share Capital	2965.03	--
Share Advance	9.99	--
Borrowings	5381.36	7253.52
Total	8356.38	7253.52
Investment in State Public Sector Undertakings	33138.79	65992.93
Break-up of organizations structure		
1. Statutory Corporation (T N Warehousing Corporation)	1	
2. Government Companies	63	
3. No. of Departmental Organisations	N.A	
4. Cooperative Organisations	N.A	
5. No. of Statutory Boards	8	

Neyveli-II, Thiagarajapuram Sakkaramangalam farms on lease basis. Besides, it developed about 60 acres of waste lands located in Amusaravakkam farm and cultivated 57.70 acres. The total extent of lands taken over from Musaravakkam, Neyveli-II, Thiagarajapuram Sakkaramangalam was 977.77 acres out of which it raised crops in the gross area of 741.46 crores.

The corporation however was not able to function on a self-supporting basis due to the following reasons:

(i) Most of the loans held by the Corporation were poramboke lands having a lot of problems like inadequate irrigation and drainage facilities which required huge expenditure of reclamation charges of levelling, bunding, etc.

(ii) The lands acquired from private persons were not normal fertility level and the soil fertility had to be built up at a huge cost.

(iii) The cost of production of foundation and certified seeds is normally high when compared to the cost of production of grain due to the additional care and attention paid in raising the crops.

(iv) In addition to the high cost of cultivation, the Corporation had to face problems like poor yield due to poor nutrient status of the soil, unproductive lands, poor productivity of labour, etc.

Since the Corporation could not function on self-supporting basis, various steps were taken to augment the financial resources. Loans were obtained from various Banks on the guarantees given by the Government to meet the administrative and cultivation expenses. Besides, the loans from banks, loans were also obtained from Market Committees and Temple funds. By July 1982, the Corporation had borrowed Rs. 253.29 lakhs from various Banks like State Bank of India, United Commercial Bank, Repatriates Cooperative Finance and Development Bank. Canara Bank and Allahabad Bank. The Corporation had also borrowed Rs. 30 lakhs from Market Committees and Temple funds. The Corporation had to pay huge amount by way of interest for the loans obtained from various Banks, Market Committees and Temple funds. To enable the Corporation to function on a self-supporting basis, the Government had to grant ways and means advances. Upto March 1982 the Corporation had obtained ways and means advances of Rs. 113 lakhs. The Corporation had also taken several steps like reduction of labour streamlining the production and marketing of seeds, etc. to reduce the losses.

Inspite of the various steps taken by the Corporation to

the Corporation on a self-supporting basis. It was found August 1982 that there was a large gap between the receipt expenditure effecting the activities of the Corporation. Even the Government provided rupees one crore every year. Corporation could not run on a self-supporting basis. All issues and problems affecting the Corporation were discussed twice by the High Level Committee. The Committee recommended to Government to wind up the activities of the Corporation to further loss.

The recommendation of the High Level Committee was carefully examined and orders were issued by the Government winding up activities of the Corporation with effect from 31.8.1982. It was also decided by the Government to take steps for the formation of Cooperative Farming Society in Neyveli Farm by the Sri Lanka Repatriates to provide employment opportunities to Sri Lanka Repatriates Labour. Training-cum-manufacturing units were attached to the Corporation which had to carry this burden without much scope to alter pattern either of the staff hierarchy or the production mix. This naturally added to the losses. Same was the case of the Tamil Nadu Ceramics. One of the major decisions of the Tamil Nadu Government which altered the situation was that of closing the unviable units even at the cost of extra retrenchment compensation to the workers. This measure, hopefully, will help these organisations to show better financial results.

There have also been cases where Corporations did not have clearcut objectives or plans of action but were started originally with vague objectives which had to be concretised over the course of time. The Tubewell Corporation, Corporation for the Economic Development of Women and Corporation for the improvement of Backward Classes are examples of this. While the Corporation for the Economic Development of Women came up with innovative schemes and overcame that handicap by means of attaching them- selves on to the various sources of funds available for development of women in the Ministry of Social Welfare or Industry, the other two are yet to organise themselves in this way.

One common strain that can be noticed in case of failure have been that the Corporations continued to function like department of the Government with perennial budgetary support helpless dependence on subsidies. It is therefore necessary that even at the formation stage the justification for an autonomous agency like a Public Sector Corporation to undertake work or develop activities has to be analysed carefully and new organisations started when these justifications are established.

TABLE 11.4

(Rupees in lakhs)

	Investment (as on 31.3.86)	*State Govt.*	*Others*
Sectorwise Classifications			
1.	Passenger Transport	15	
2.	Other Transport (engaged in movement of cargo)	2	
3.	Engineering (ancillary to Transport Corporation engaged in Tyre Retreading and other works related to Passenger Transport)	3	
4.	Manufacturing	8	
5.	Mining	2	
6.	Trading	2	
7.	Development Finance	8	
8.	Promotional	8	
9.	Agriculture & Allied activities	6	
10.	Construction	4	
11.	Miscellaneous (including T.N. Warehousing Corporation)	5	

TABLE 11.5

Profit and Loss Position of All the State Public Sector Undertakings

(61 P.S.U. mentioned in Item No. (iii) infra)

		1983-84	1984-85	1985-86
(a)	Cash Profit	1184.09	2565.42	9048.36
(b)	Depreciation	3696.93	4338.61	8304.81
(c)	Gross Profit	(-) 2512.84	(-) 1773.19	(+) 743.55
(d)	Investment	2659.36	3946.94	7413.78
(e)	Net Profit (after tax)	(-) 5349.71	(-) 5965.46	(-) 6910.99

TABLE 11.6

Sectorwise Net Profit and Loss Position

(before prior period adjustment)

(Rupees in Lakhs)

	1983-84	1984-85	1985-86
Passenger Transport	(-) 998.27	(-) 299.93	(+) 253.91
Other Transport	(+) 30.83	(+) 43.21	(+)158.80
Engineering	(+) 5.84	(+) 5.89	(+) 6.92
Manufacturing	(-) 226.98	(-) 675.25	(-) 3013.02
Mining	(+) 18.18	18.14	(-) 33.33
Trading	(-) 4659.24	(-) 5686.59	(-) 4762.92
Development Finance (India)	(+) 369.02	(+) 529.21	(+) 403.28
Promotional	(+) 0.52	(+) 16.90	(-) 15.61
Agriculture & Allied activities	(+) 125.79	(-) 4.37	(-) 92.17
Construction	(-) 145.64	(-) 63.46	(+) 41.11
Miscellaneous	(+) 88.80	(+) 107.39	(+) 168.72

Status of SLPEs in Tamil Nadu

The Table 11.7 presents the status of SLPEs as on March 31st 2005.

TABLE 11.7

Status of SLPEs in Tamil Nadu

(Rs. in Crores)

Years *Items*	*1999-00*	*2000-01*	*2001-02*	*2002-03*	*2003-04*
1. Total no. of SLPEs	84	82	82	82	82
2. No.of Working SLPEs	72	70	70	70	70
3. No.of Non-Working SLPEs	12	12	12	12	12
(i) Under liquidation	1				
(ii) Under Closure	10				
(iii) Under Merger	1				
(iv) Others					
4. Total Equity	1819.22	1732.56	1732.56	1732.56	1732.56
5. Total Debt	8338.58	7962.01	7962.01	7962.01	7962.01
6. Total Investment	10157.8	9694.57	9694.57	9694.57	9694.57
7. No. of Profit making enterprises	30	34	34	34	34
8. No. of Loss making enterprises	50	47	47	47	47
9. Net Profit/Loss	-64.75	77.91	77.91	77.91	77.91
10. Accumulated Loss(-)/Profit	676.33	967.49	967.49	967.49	967.49

Source: Reports of the Comptroller and Auditor General of India (Commercial), on Tamil Nadu for 1999-00 to 2003-04.

Index